Sparking Curiosity through Project-Based Learning in the Early Childhood Classroom

Learn how to tap into and illuminate the creative potential in all learners with this inspiring and practical book. This book teaches educators to unlock the creativity in all learners while celebrating inquiry at its highest levels. Each chapter explores how to create learning spaces that invite deep inquiry, initiate thoughtful conversations, invite wonder and curiosity in learning each day, and maintain high levels of engagement. The approachable framework is built around the three-phase project model and is broken down into a user-friendly planning tool, explaining how to approach project-based teaching and learning in any early childhood classroom. Coupled with noteworthy true stories, sample units, and example pictures, early childhood educators will come away with tools and plans to enhance teaching and learning practices in their classroom through a project-based approach.

Elizabeth Hoyle Konecni is an educator from New Orleans, Louisiana, and currently works as an educational consultant. She has served in various roles in her many years in education, including classroom teacher, administrator, curriculum specialist, and instructional coach.

T0383435

Sparking Curiosity through Project-Based Learning in the Early Childhood Classroom

Strategies and Tools to Unlock Student Potential

Elizabeth Hoyle Konecni

Routledge
Taylor & Francis Group

NEW YORK AND LONDON

First published 2023
by Routledge
605 Third Avenue, New York, NY 10158

and by Routledge
4 Park Square, Milton Park, Abingdon, Oxon, OX14 4RN

Routledge is an imprint of the Taylor & Francis Group, an informa business

ISBN: 978-1-032-36538-1 (hbk)
ISBN: 978-1-032-35507-8 (pbk)
ISBN: 978-1-003-33254-1 (ebk)

DOI: 10.4324/9781003332541

Typeset in Palatino
by SPi Technologies India Pvt Ltd (Straive)

Access the Support Material: www.routledge.com/9781032355078

Dedicated to my beautiful mother
The most wonderful teacher of them all!

Contents

Acknowledgments

There are many amazing people that have made this book possible, and to each of them, I extend open arms of gratitude.

A huge thank you to my amazing family! Thank you for the constant love, support and joy. Thank you for making our nightly dinners a memory I'll cherish forever!

Scott, I love you! Thank you for being my partner in life.

Thank you, Mama and Daddy, for lighting the spark of teaching and learning in all three children! We love what we do! Thank you for being the best mom and dad.

Tyler and Ella, thank you for showing me the true joy in play! I am grateful for the happiness you bring to every single day!

Amy, you are truly the most amazing person I know! Thank you for always being my thought partner. I love you.

John, thank you for pressing the mute button on me all those years ago! It's a memory I'll treasure and never forget. I'm grateful for your expertise as a learner, a teacher and, most importantly, as an incredible writer.

Charlotte, designer extraordinaire, thank you for all your behind-the-scenes help!

Wonderful and fantastic Elliott, what would anyone do without you? Thank you for always checking after me and correcting my overabundance of comma errors.

Precious Andrea, thank you for being an illuminating light with an unwavering faith! I am forever grateful to you!

Amazing Maria, I cried the first time I sat in your professional development because you made me question everything about my teaching craft, and, for that, I am most grateful! Thank you for showing me the joys of life-long learning! I'm forever grateful for your impact on my teaching career!

A special thanks goes to Kirsch, an amazing leader, and the wonderful Early Childhood team at Holy Name of Jesus. Thank you for your willingness to take on project-based learning (PBL)! You amaze me every time I visit! You have cultivated incredible project-based learning environments! I have loved every minute of working with you, and I'm excited about the next PBL units we'll build together.

I'm forever grateful to generous Melanie for sharing her learning space with me. Brighter Horizons is a magnificent place to learn and grow. Thank you for welcoming me into your joy-filled classroom! I love watching the happiness of teaching and learning come to life in your classroom. Your spirit of constant generosity is contagious.

Thank you, Carol, for the endless hours you put into editing this book! I am grateful for your kindness and expertise.

Denise, my beautiful best friend, thank you for always being ready to talk teaching and learning. I will always be grateful for our friendship.

Most importantly, to every student, co-worker, teacher, and friend, it was through every moment spent working and learning alongside you that the idea for this book was possible. Thank you for inspiring and teaching me about the love of learning!

I am grateful to be a Routledge author! Nicole and Olivia, thank you for guiding me every step of the way! It has been a joy working with you.

1

Project-Based Learning and Your Inner Child

What's your very best memory of playing as a child … the one that grabs your attention and brings a smile to your face? Do you remember the joy you felt using your imagination or creating something new?

My childhood memories of play include enormous messes paired with a zest for inventing. My creations led to me pull out every item from our hall closets as I skillfully built tents with the sheets off my parent's bed. I designed houses in the bushes complete with our fine China from the highest cabinets in the kitchen. But my personal favorite creation was a giant classroom in our family's two-car garage. I would spend hours at a time lost in my own imagination.

There was joy!
There was creativity!
There was motivation!
There was learning!

DOI: 10.4324/9781003332541-1

FIGURE 1.1 Illustration of classroom set up in a garage.

I can step back into these moments like it was yesterday. I made my parents back their cars out of the garage every weekend, so I could have room to build. My classroom had an enormous teacher's desk made of cardboard boxes, complete with a name tag with Miss Elizabeth scribbled across the front.

FIGURE 1.2 Illustration of girl holding nametag over eyes.

The students' desks were made of milk crates and pieces of scrap wood from under my dad's workbench.

Outfitting my classroom was an adventure. Since both of my parents were teachers, we didn't have a whole lot of money growing up. Every Saturday morning, our family would pile into the car and spend a few hours visiting local garage sales. I was too embarrassed to be seen at second-hand sales, so I stayed in the car and sent my dad with a list of classroom supplies. While the entire family exited the car, I slowly slid down the backseat and made my way onto the floorboard of the car. Then, I'd wrap my arms around my head, praying that no one would see me at the garage sale. It was the same scenario every single Saturday morning. My dad would circle the local sales in the paper, we'd pile in our family car, we'd drive to each sale, they'd leave the car and I'd slump down hiding with sheer embarrassment. A few minutes later, the family would come back to the car, I'd wait for my dad to drive off and then I'd slowly make my way up the back seat. He'd tell me about all the things that he found for my pretend classroom. Then, we'd pull back in the driveway and unload all the new treasures for my classroom.

FIGURE 1.3 Illustration of girl hiding in backseat of car.

Once, I asked my dad to look for a chalkboard. He thought that this would be impossible to find. To my surprise, as I was trembling with embarrassment on the floorboard of the car one Saturday morning, without telling me he loaded up a huge chalkboard in the trunk of our car. It was so large the trunk wouldn't close. I wondered why we were riding with the trunk popped, and my dad just kept talking in circles, refusing to let the secret out. Once we pulled into our driveway, my dad rushed inside with the new treasure. As I walked in the front door, he put his two hands over my eyes like a blindfold and led me to the garage. When my foot stepped down onto the garage floor, he slowly moved his hands to reveal my best surprise: an enormous chalkboard. This memory is so vivid in my mind. I can still feel the excitement of seeing that chalkboard. I can still feel the wheels of my mind turning with ideas for creating and building in my classroom. I didn't know it at the time, but my curiosity about classrooms, learning more about what teachers do, and the intricate set-up of a classroom, was my introduction to project-based learning.

I hope your memories of adventurous and fearless play still bring a smile to your face also. Our childhood is filled with wonder, curiosity and discovery. We learned about the world through play. There weren't any worksheets to fill out, computer programs for goal-reaching or chairs to warm. No, this space was solely for inventing, creating and taking risks. I've come to learn that if we as teachers want true engagement in our lessons, especially our lessons in early childhood classrooms, then we have to reach back into our childhood memories of play and learn more from our younger selves.

What did we think about? How did we learn? What was important? How did we stay curious about the world around us?

This is exactly what our students crave as young learners, to see the world through the lens of curiosity. In this role, they become fearless learners that wonder about the world around them.

When I was a teacher, I didn't always know what this looked like, especially in early childhood education. In my current work as an instructional coach for teachers and principals, I'm still met with various challenges that I don't always know the answer to. During these moments in my job, I revert to my childhood memories and step into that childlike thinking mindset from when I was fearless!

When I was a child I wasn't scared to make and learn from my mistakes. It was OK that I didn't know all the answers because I knew if I kept looking and trying on new ideas, I'd figure out an answer to my wonder. This is the mindset I strive to embrace as a coach.

One summer a principal friend called and asked if I'd be willing to take on introducing and implementing project-based learning in her early childhood department. She voiced that she truly wanted to transition out so many worksheets and move play-based learning into the framework of their academic program. I joyfully accepted the challenge!

After we hung up, sheer panic hit me! I wasn't quite sure that I knew enough about play-based learning or how I was going to go about teaching it to an entire early childhood department. After taking a few minutes to compose myself, I sat down and drafted a plan. First on my list was to spend the entire summer researching best practices in play-based learning. I knew it was going to be a challenge, but at the time, I had no idea how much I was going to learn and how this would forever change the trajectory of my beliefs in teaching and learning.

That summer I spent every waking moment researching, trying on and reflecting. I read many books in early childhood play-based education, watched videos, scoured the internet for thought-provoking articles and soaked in all my new learning. After that deep dive into learning more about project-based learning in the classroom, I was confident

a. that I had enough background knowledge to build curriculum and professional development around this project;

    b. that my entire summer was spent learning more about how early learners view the world;

    c. that my views about early childhood education were rapidly changing; and

    d. that learning through play was a rigorous part of project-based learning.

In August I was greeted by a team of about twenty-five teachers and assistants ready to learn more about project-based learning and its role in their classrooms. I arrived ready to share this new learning. We watched TED talks, read articles, took part in meaningful conversations, learned more about play and its role in the early childhood classroom and began planning our first project-based unit. What I didn't realize was that this was just the jump-start to the important learning that we'd watch take place over the next few years. I've learned so much from that initial summer of intense studying and that first professional development session, and I'd love to unfold my findings in the next few chapters of this book. The goal of this book is to frame what truly engages our young learners and how we can bring more of that true engagement into our classroom environments each day.

Chapter 1 Reflection

What is your best memory of childhood play?

How did you feel when you were playing?

What learning opportunities can you gain from that memory and apply right back into your classroom or school?

Did play feel different than sitting in your classroom? Explain.

Bridge Building 101 – Learning from the Childlike Mindset

FIGURE 1.4 Child using blocks to build a bridge.

What qualities did this child use in his bridge creation?

What might stop you now, as an adult, from trying to build this?

What barriers are you facing that would need to be dropped?

Further Reading

Beneke, S, Ostrosky, M. M., & Katz, L. G. (2018). *The project approach for all learners: A hands-on guide for inclusive early childhood classrooms* (1st ed.). Brookes Publishing.

Kogan, Y., Chard, S., & Castillo, C. A. (2017). *Picturing the project approach: Creative explorations in early learning*. Gryphon House.

Laur, D., & Ackers, J. (2017). *Developing natural curiosity through project-based learning: Five strategies for the Prek-3 classroom*. Routledge.

Lev, S. (2020). *Implementing project based learning in early childhood* (1st ed.). Routledge.

Mraz, K., Porcelli, A., & Tyler, C. (2016). *Purposeful play: A teacher's guide to igniting deep and joyful learning across the day* (Illustrated ed.). Heinemann.

Stacey, S. (2018). *Inquiry-based early learning environments: Creating, supporting, and collaborating* (Illustrated ed.). Redleaf Press.

2

Shifting Thinking

When I was young, my older brother and sister pestered me to no end. At times, it was brutal. One night, when I was seven years old, I admit that I was being especially annoying to my older siblings by screaming nonstop so they couldn't hear the television show they were watching. It bothered me that they were watching TV because I wanted them to play with me. Since they weren't interested in playing, I found a surefire way to get their attention. Well, it turns out, they wouldn't let me get the last laugh. My very brilliant brother wasn't going to be outdone by his annoying little sister. He quickly picked up the remote and said in his calmest brotherly voice, "I'm just going to mute you," and with that, he forcefully pressed down on the mute button. As you can imagine, this infuriated me! I began screaming even louder. My sister and brother proceeded to have a peaceful conversation between themselves. They said, "It looks like she might be trying to tell us something, too bad we can't hear her." I was outraged! Then I became worried that they really couldn't hear me. They were so convincing that I truly believed they controlled my voice and couldn't hear me. After about five minutes of continual screaming, I finally gave up and walked away, thinking that my brother and sister could mute me at any time with the television remote control.

DOI: 10.4324/9781003332541-2

I spent the next few months believing that my siblings could mute my voice with the television remote control. Being the smallest voice in the family, I had become used to screaming to get my brother's and sister's attention. This tried and tested strategy abruptly ended. I knew I would have to shift attention-getting practices. Be assured that I found many new ways to pester them. I won't bother listing all my new strategies because I still use them today, when necessary! But trust me, a new perspective can lead to innovative practices. This was true for me as a child and is equally true in our classrooms.

NASA's Findings

One piece of research that I find incredible, started with a question from NASA about some of their team members. Scientists were trying to measure the creative ability in NASA engineers and rocket scientists. In other words, what made them tick? What made these scientists think at high levels of superior creativity? A research project would soon bring to light new information about the way learners are molded into thinking processes throughout their years of schooling.

In the late 1960s, NASA hired Dr. George Land and Dr. Beth Jarman to create and administer a test that would carefully analyze creative ability and its source. Their findings, to this day, are still astounding and illuminate what even our youngest children need in their early years in the classroom.

Dr. Land and Dr. Jarman began the study by evaluating approximately 1,600 four- and five-year-old children. The test assessed their ability to problem solve as they thought up new and innovative solutions to problems. Guess how many scored at the genius level?

A **surprising** 98% of the tested group scored at the creative genius level.

The scientists were shocked at the findings and decided to launch a longitudinal study. They evaluated the identical group of children five years later; the results were discouraging. The same children were no longer at the top of the ranking as they were five years prior. The staggering 98% creative genius level now fell to just 30%. What happened to the other 68%? Did they just stop being geniuses?

Researchers tested the same group once more five years later, and yet again, the percentage had fallen, from 30% to only 12%. Consider this: over a ten-year time span, the tested children's scores declined from 98% scoring at the creative genius level at age five to 12% scoring at the creative genius level at age 15.

Can 86% of the identified creative geniuses suddenly decline into average ability levels?

Can one grow out of being a genius?

In their final test, researchers tested the population in adulthood and the original 98% figure had now gone down to 2% over a period of 20 years. What happened to these creative thinkers? (Land and Jarman, 1992)

TABLE 2.1

Data supported by Drs. Land and Jarman portraying creative abilities from age 4 to adulthood

Longitudinal Study on Creative Ability	
Age Tested	Percent Scoring at Creative Genius Level (%)
5	98
10	30
15	12
Adult (25 and up)	2

Shocking, isn't it?

I still have to take a deep breath every time I review the data.

The Findings

So, what exactly did this research lead Drs. Land and Jarman to find? They concluded that "non-creative behavior is learned." – Land

Essentially, our youngest learners come to us as creative geniuses, and over time in school and exposure to social stereotypes and convergent thinking, children lose their creative spark. As Sir Ken Robinson noted in a famous TED Talk, "Do Schools Kill Creativity?," "all kids have tremendous talents, and we squander them pretty ruthlessly" (TED, 2006). His brilliant take on how we are slowly removing every ounce of creativity in our classrooms focuses a new lens on our early childhood classrooms. Our classrooms begin to define learning and set lifelong expectations of how classrooms function. He goes on to share this study from NASA conducted by Drs. Land and Jarman.

Do our traditional classroom models limit children by taking away their ability to deeply ponder the world around them? As a teacher, I am always reflecting and questioning my beliefs and experiences. Reflective questions that guide my practice include:

◆ How do we create life-long learners?
◆ Do I stifle learning in my classroom? How might I be stifling creativity?
◆ What are the outcomes that I want for my students?
◆ What am I doing for children that they can do independently?
◆ Am I allowing for open-ended thinking or am I looking for a specific answer?
◆ What is true problem solving and what does it look like?

After considering these questions to reflect on my own teaching practices, I was able to shift my perspective and embark on a new educational journey. I discovered that project-based learning (PBL) was a successful approach to honor student creativity and wonder while building deep knowledge. Taking a PBL approach required a shift in my thinking. Change is never easy, but it becomes much more manageable when we are intentional from the onset.

Shifting into New Views

SHIFT ONE – Be Clear about Engagement

True engagement happens when students are intrinsically motivated to learn more about their own interests and passions. Students experience ownership in their learning when they are interested and engaged.

Not all children are necessarily interested in learning about the same things and, likewise, neither are adults. I'm not superinterested in sports, especially football. There I said it, like me or not, I just am not into sports. My father, sister, brother, brother in-law, husband and many others around me love sports. They love to watch games, talk about plays and even play in fantasy leagues. I find this to be a complete waste of time. In my mind, I could be doing many more productive things rather than wasting two and a half hours watching a boring old football game. They, however, see this as an exciting way to spend a Sunday afternoon. If my family made me watch a football game, I'd be pretty angry. Their idea of making me watch the game just hoping I'll eventually be captivated just wouldn't work. I'm just not into football.

Now, if they approached this in a different manner and said, "Liz, we're watching the football game this afternoon. Would you like to watch it with us? During the game we could talk about Drew Brees's contributions to education."

This approach speaks to me, because while I despise football, I love talking about education. And maybe, just maybe, I might learn to tolerate football through talking about what players are doing for the wonderful world of education. So instead of making me sit and watch the game because they like it, it's a way for us to all be together, connected to one core idea but moving forward in our own interests.

Part of our important role as teachers is to unite our students' interests about a topic as we move forward together as an entire community of learners.

Lens on Engagement – A Glimpse of a Lesson Uniting
All Learning Interests Centered Around One Topic

FIGURE 2.1 Neighborhood made of shoeboxes.

In this photo, one can see that students' areas of interest can all be honored under the umbrella of almost any unit topic and should become visible through their work. In a project-based unit on houses, students investigate the styles and purposes of many different home designs from around the world, for example, an apartment, adobe style and a castle just to name a few. Students become experts in home design becoming an expert in a specific type of home through analyzing photographs, reading informational texts and partaking in deep conversations with peers. Then, they design their own home and build a 3D model of their design. Students display their knowledge through the details they include in their build and share their expertise in individual presentations. It's important that the entire class invest their learning in homes around the world; however, individual final products represent their interests.

Project-based learning offers interest choice to learners while intrinsically motivating students to master the standard, whereas thematic units are limited to a one-way learning outcome. In a thematic unit, the teacher may see a cut and paste of a house, a coloring sheet or a possible creation where all students work toward a product that looks exactly same the same. In project-based learning, students learn alongside the teacher and their peers while they work within their area of interest and share their expert knowledge. In looking at both instructional methods, it's important to consider what you value in teaching and learning and what is best for your students. If you find yourself contemplating how to incorporate PBL into your current thematic units, rest easy, because this is something you can gradually do until you find your classroom fully immersed in PBL.

SHIFT TWO – It's Time to Lose the Control

We don't have (and can't) control each moment of learning.

In my early years as a school administrator, I can remember the hallways of my school lined with student work. I paid special attention to this work because I felt it was a window into a child's thinking. In one classroom, students were learning about apples, and their student work hung on the wall outside their classroom. After passing the seventh paper, I realized that every single paper looked exactly the same. As I kept walking, my eyes remained glued to these red, yellow and green dots on apple trees. Every single dot was perfectly placed in just about the same spot on the tree on twenty pieces of paper. I often wonder how this looked in the classroom. Did the teacher point to the exact spot on the tree to place each sticker, or were they prelabeled with the students just following directions in this activity? What was the learning target that day, and was it achieved? Who owned the work? Who carried the cognitive lift?

While this is an extreme example of control in a classroom, it's also a clear picture of the fear we have in losing control of our classroom. Whether we're sticking colored apples on a tree, planning our next themed unit, or teaching a handwriting activity, I think we can all agree that we control too many learning opportunities in our classrooms. As teachers, we often think that we must maintain a certain type of control in our classroom, or our students won't learn, and the class would then get out of hand. Yes, we should absolutely have well-managed classrooms; however, this control may look different than it has in the past. We must let go of the fact that our students need us to tell them how to do every little thing and step into the new image of ourselves cultivating learners that thrive on independent problem solving.

Releasing control may be one of the biggest shifts in mindset that teachers have when moving toward a project-based approach. It's hard for us to step back because we feel like we'll lose control of our well-managed classroom. Throughout this book, we'll learn how to release learning to the students so they can investigate and discover as they make connections and share their learning with the classroom community.

Lens on Dropping the Control – A Glimpse Into Classrooms That Cultivate Independent Problem Solvers

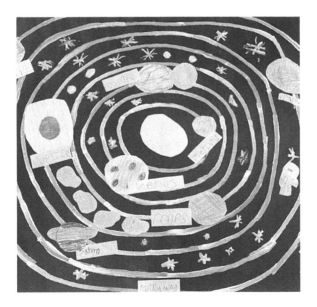

FIGURE 2.2 Solar system mural.

This photo features a glimpse of our solar system and the many parts and pieces that comprise our vast space. The teacher has cultivated an environment where students are well-equipped to think independently, converse, and share their knowledge through group or independent projects. In this mural, the entire class worked together to display its collective knowledge on the solar system. The project started as a blank piece of large black paper. The teacher simply posed a question, provided the needed materials and supported students as they brought the solar system to life in a large mural. The mural hung outside of their classroom in the hallway for the entire school to share in their learned knowledge. What if the teacher would have controlled this mural? What might the outcome look like? What would be the knowledge gained by the learner?

SHIFT THREE – Step into Your Students' World

Foster a love for learning by cultivating an environment where deep thinking is joyful.

Be the change.

Imagine yourself as the catalyst in the classroom. Acting boldly, you can quickly create a PBL environment for students to explore and thrive. Here's an important question to ask ourselves as we ponder our role as a catalyst: How are we impacting change in learning behaviors?

Once I was visiting a group of kindergarten teachers to check in on the progress of their latest project on weather patterns. These teachers had been immersed in project teaching for two years at that time, and they were on their way to becoming master project teachers. As I entered the classrooms, I found a variety of high-quality teaching and learning practices sprinkled around the classroom. In one area, students were observing the weather from the window and jotting notes and drawings about their observations in their weather journals. In another part of the classroom, students created a weather station and were taking turns as young meteorologists sharing the weather and its expected patterns over the next few days. In a third corner of the room, students were taking on the role of sky watchers as they carefully analyzed pictures of different types of weather, had conversations with their peers about its patterns, and then painted an expression of weather with watercolor.

"Where was the teacher?," you may ask. This is the beauty of project-based teaching and learning: she wasn't with a specific group, nor was she acting as an information giver. She was moving around the room with a binder and pen in hand. Her role at this moment was to observe her students' findings, as she documented what she observed in each student. Sometimes she would kneel down to ask probing questions of her eager researchers, commenting on one of their findings or sharing an idea that learners had discussed with the rest of the class. In these moments, she had embraced her role as a catalyst for her learners. She had changed the action of learning in a few short months. In the previous school year, I can recall a markedly different unit on weather which consisted of a multitude of teacher-led activities, resulting in the final products looking the same for each child.

Sometimes we get caught up in a cycle of using packets or activities, because we're not sure how to elevate the teaching and learning in our classroom. As teachers, it is essential to step back and reflect upon our impact on learning and engagement. During this reflection process, it is powerful to empathize with our students and look at the classroom experience through their perspective.

Lens on Stepping Into Our Students' World – A Glimpse Into Cultivating Joy in Learning by Being the Change

The following examples highlight the pure joy of learning through investigative research and discovery. In one classroom, the veteran teacher had never taught with the project approach until her unit on cultures this year. We planned a step-by-step unit with her team, and she embraced this new model of teaching and learning. She served as a catalyst in her classroom for her students as well as her entire pre-K team of teachers. Teachers across the school were looking to her for guidance and support even after her first PBL unit. Students led the learning, and the teacher provided supports for their learning journey. As they uncovered more about the Chinese culture, she continued to encourage their curiosity. Instead of coloring a premade map of the world, she provided pictures of the Earth, a discussion about land and water, and as a class they located China and the United States on a globe. Then, she provided blue and green play dough and invited students to create the Earth and show China and its relation to the United States. As her students created their models, she questioned, initiated lively discussions, and provided pictorial supports for their creations. As the unit progressed, the class discovered more about how the Chinese culture celebrates the new year. After studying the celebration, the students planned, created, and threw their own Chinese New Year celebration. Students took part in creating a life-sized dragon and paraded around the school to share their knowledge and learning with other grade levels.

SHIFT FOUR – You're Not the Only Expert in the Room

In my early years of teaching, the district I worked for adopted a new reading curriculum, and our grade level was selected to pilot it. Part of the piloting process included our grade-level team observing demonstration lessons given by the large textbook company in order to demonstrate effective use of their curriculum. I remember not really liking this new curriculum, because it felt so, well… rehearsed.

One morning, my entire team, along with central office personnel, were observing a demonstration lesson on vocabulary. I was seated at a long table toward the back of the classroom. There were a few empty seats at the table. Each member of the central office grabbed a chair, and the lesson began.

I remember the demonstrator reading a short four-paragraph story aloud to the students as they sat on the carpet in the front of the room. The demonstrator from the textbook company was the only person with a copy of the text, and the students' role was to listen to the story. After finishing reading the story aloud, she focused on certain words in the text that may have been seen as difficult. It was a vocabulary demonstration from the scripted curriculum, the demonstrator's role was to show us how to effectively teach vocabulary to our students.

The vocabulary lesson continued with repeating one of the words in the text and then giving the definition to the class aloud.

Then, the definition was repeated a second time and the students were asked to chorally recite it back.

I remember asking myself, "I wonder what will happen next?"

But… there were no next steps. That was it. Say the word and repeat the definition.

That was the demonstration lesson. We'd all been called together to observe how to memorize definitions.

One fellow observer turned to toward me with a smile and said, "Wasn't that amazing?" I turned back and without thinking before the words could roll off my tongue, I responded "But students just regurgitated the definitions, they didn't even do any thinking." When I realized that those words had made it out of my mouth, I gulped. I peered down at the floor and then brought my eyes to her level. She wasn't pleased with my answer.

While that probably wasn't the best thing to say, this memory remains forever embedded in my mind. In that moment, we were being trained to be the sole information givers in our classroom. This isn't anyone's fault, but, oftentimes, we fall into this trap. I know I can honestly say I've fallen into the trap quite a few times in my teaching career. In that defining moment, I realized it was time for a shift in the student's role as learner, not just as information receiver.

As we reflect together on that demonstration lesson, from my early years in teaching, we realize that the students were responsible for little to no thinking work. Their role in that learning moment was to memorize a definition then recite it back. This is not where true learning happens. Our students need to take part in a productive struggle throughout the learning process. It's important for students to question the world around them and find answers to their own questions.

Let's fast-forward 15 years later into a student-centered vocabulary experience that happened in a pre-K classroom, an experience that shows the power of the teacher stepping out of the sole information giver role, and into a facilitator role.

The students are learning about flowers in their project study. They have taken nature walks, observed flowers, investigated different parts of a flower, planted varieties and now they're deepening their understanding of a flower and a flower's role in the environment. As the students begin reading and research-ing independently and as a whole group, unfamiliar words pop up throughout their learning experiences. Instead of the teacher placing prewritten definitions on a vocabulary wall or simply providing the students with her definition, she takes an entirely different approach.

The students have taken on the role of information seekers. As they come across words that they don't know the meaning of, they investigate to search for a deeper understanding of it sometimes in whole-group learning and sometimes in indepen-dent inquiry. The students bring the words to the teacher, along with their student-friendly understanding of its meaning. The teacher then writes the word at the top of a sheet of paper, if the child is unable to legibly write the word. It's the learner's role to draw their student-friendly definition under the word. The new word is placed on the vocabulary wall and the student shares her findings with the rest of the class. As the unit progresses, the vocabulary wall grows with words that the students find in their discoveries.

FIGURE 2.3 Vocabulary on focus wall featuring student drawn definitions.

The students are eager to seek out information and share their findings with the rest of their class community. This method of teaching vocabulary gives ownership to the learner, cultivates a life-long process of word investigation and values their research findings.

Lens on Leaving the Role of Sole Information Giver – A Glimpse Into the Role of Facilitator

FIGURE 2.4 Teacher working with small group.

Nancie, a second-year pre-K 4 teacher, believes in the project-based approach. She has fully embraced the facilitator role in her classroom and her students are blossoming. As you carefully analyze her facial expressions, you can see that she is joyful about supporting her learners in their quests about discovering more about the world around them. She is seated at a table with four students. The students are pulling apart flowers, noticing and having conversations about their findings. Nancie is supporting her students through guiding questions and deepening the conversation. She has stepped away from the role of sole information giver and into the role of facilitator. She has provided her students with materials to support their learning journey and encourages them as they grow in their knowledge about the world around them.

FIGURE 2.5 Students investigating the parts of a flower.

SHIFT FIVE – Silence is Toxic

In the early years of my teaching career, I felt vivacious, daring and ready to teach my little heart out. One clear memory stands out as I think back on the idea of productive and purposeful student-centered conversations. My principal had come to my classroom one afternoon to share the news that the state superintendent would be visiting our school the next day to tour and visit four classrooms on our school campus; mine would be one of the four. I was nervous and excited at the same time. I immediately started planning what I thought was going to be an amazing lesson in writing. We had been working on narratives, and I wanted him to see what my students were producing.

The next afternoon came quickly; the state superintendent and his team were set to walk through my classroom door any minute. I taught a model lesson to my eager writers and sent them off to write independently. The room was completely silent as I walked around the room checking in on my writers. I just knew when he walked in that he would be amazed at my management style and the construction of narrative writing the students were producing. Today I am so grateful that I never had the opportunity to meet that state superintendent that afternoon. As I look back now, he would have probably been so disappointed in what he saw; I know I am.

To my good fortune, New Orleans traffic slowed him down so that he didn't make it to all our classrooms before dismissal. Thank goodness! I now know that the silence I demanded in my room stifled creativity. It created isolated thinking bubbles that did not allow for collaboration and connections.

Productive conversations among students of all ability levels supports them as they try on, manipulate and master content. It's through their deep conversations and questions to their peers that they begin making those connections. In this book we'll build an understanding around how to cultivate purposeful conversations that drive the learning forward.

As my brother and sister proved, a mute button was the best way to bring silence into the room so they could carry on with their show. Both hilarious and thought-provoking, my family's story can be a deeper glimpse into the world of a child's mind. That mute button meant that my voice didn't matter, and they were in complete control of me.

What are we silencing in our learners? What do we unknowingly mute in each child's thinking and learning processes? How can we begin to feel comfortable unmuting our children, as we step into their world of learning and enhance our teaching and learning practices with inquiry, discovery and joy?

Lens on Cultivating Productive Classroom Conversations – A Glimpse Into Illuminating Conversations

Pre-K4 students are sharing their ideas as they compare the familiar "Cinderella" (2022) story by Marcia Brown (2022) to the Chinese version, "Yeh-Shen" by Ai-Ling Louie (1996). They are caught up in conversation about the characters in each story. It was delightful to hear their thinking, as they built on each other's ideas. In this classroom, conversation is the heart of the room. Students are welcome to converse with each other often about their learning. They are comfortable sharing ideas, questioning one another, and correcting an idea if it seems unclear or incorrect. Students are driving their own learning forward as they compare the two fairy tales and deepen their understanding of character traits and story elements.

FIGURE 2.6 Comparison chart of Yeh-Shen and Cinderella.

Wrapping It Up

These five shifts support students in reaching their highest levels of learning through authentic engagement. Consider each shift and how it may impact the decisions made in your teaching and learning environments. We're all constantly reflecting on our teaching practices as we continuously strive to reach each learner and support them on in their individualized learning journey.

Chapter 2 Reflection

What shift is remaining in your thought box?
How might you slowly begin bringing a few of these shifts into your classroom environment?

Becoming an Ant Expert – Learning from the Childlike Mindset

FIGURE 2.7 Child's artwork displays the knowledge learned in a study on ants.

What shifts must the teacher have embraced to support the learner in this project?

What do you think happens each time this child steps outside and finds an ant?

References

Do schools kill creativity? | Sir Ken Robinson. (2007, January 7). YouTube. https://www.youtube.com/watch?v=iG9CE55wbtY

Land, G., & Jarman, B. (1992). *Breakpoint and beyond: Mastering the future today*. HarperBusiness.

TEDxTucson George Land The Failure Of Success. (2011, February 16). YouTube. https://www.youtube.com/watch?v=ZfKMq-rYtnc

Picture Book References

Brown, M. (2022). *Cinderella*. Atheneum Books for Young Readers.

Louie, A. (1996). *Yeh-Shen: A Cinderella story from China* (1st ed.). Puffin Books.

3

A Plannable Framework

In the beginning stages of planning, project-based learning (PBL) can feel like a daunting task for a teacher, no matter how experienced they may be. I don't cook much and for novice chefs like me, planning a PBL unit would be like trying to cook gumbo. I wouldn't even know where to begin. Should I start with a roux, maybe not? Should I add shrimp or leave the seafood behind and bring chicken and sausage into the spotlight? The mere thought of cooking gumbo is frightening! There are unforeseen steps, tricky timing and, worst of all, gumbo enthusiasts just waiting to critique the final bowl. Similarly, just as gumbo may seem to be a dauting task for beginners in the kitchen, project-based learning in its infant stages can seem intimidating to early childhood teachers. When you visualize all the pieces of great PBL lessons, it's hard to imagine where to begin. How do I plan for engaging each child? How do I know if I'm leading children down the right path?

Embracing PBL means empowering students. Releasing responsibility and control to students can be scary. This chapter offers a framework for your planning to ensure that students are engaged in purposeful learning. And before you know it, releasing responsibility and control will become the most joyful part of your teaching day.

Mastering PBL means trying it out and seeing what works with your students. It's about jumping in feet first and allowing your students to jump in right next to you. PBL takes away

DOI: 10.4324/9781003332541-3

the idea that we, the teacher, must be the sole information giver and every child's work should look exactly alike. It's liberating to shift from traditional thought models of teaching and immerse yourself in PBL! So, pack away your worries and anxieties about PBL and embrace the joyful planning process.

Framing the Work

Beautiful paintings are frequently encased in a picture frame that serves as a structure or boundary between the art and the wall. It helps to think of our planning process as the structure around the brilliant work our students will do in a PBL lesson.

As we plan the instructional goals and outcomes of each unit, we'll be working within a project frame that sits invisibly around the exciting learning taking place in the classroom. This frame acts as a guide to support the unit in its entirety. It provides a starting point for planning and a structure that can be applied in every project unit you write.

In this chapter we'll cultivate an understanding of the three phases of a complete PBL unit and the role each phase plays within the PBL framework. Just like a gumbo pot frames a variety of gumbo ingredients inside, the project framework acts as the gumbo pot, supporting the planning of each project topic. It allows many creative ideas to take shape within the project, while giving structure through a step-by-step progression.

Working in a Three-Phase Framework

The planning framework allows you to lean into your own sense of wonder and creativity as you plan units. There are no stringent rules that say you must do this now and this later. You have the autonomy to consider what activities will invite high levels of inquiry and discovery throughout the entire unit. The framework simply supports a natural progression of the learning process.

When eating gumbo in New Orleans, one might wonder why there are so many different types. In one restaurant alone, you might see three different types of gumbo on the menu. There are endless recipes for creating the perfect pot of gumbo. I'd say the same about planning a project-based unit. There are endless possibilities that lead to successful projects in early childhood classrooms.

The PBL framework includes three phases into the planning and creation of each project unit. Within each phase, the roles of the teacher and learner shift as the project progresses, inviting learners to take on the role of lead learner in their area of expertise. Each phase builds upon the prior phase and the work that happened within the phase. The learner and learning could not progress to the next phase without first spending time in the previous phase. Let's carefully look at each phase, its purpose, and the progression it leads to in the next phase within the framework.

PBL Project Framework: A Guide to Planning

TABLE 3.1
Visual of the three phases of project-based learning

Topic Selection Webbing	Phase One	Phase Two	Phase Three
	→→→→→→→→→→→→→→→→→→→→→→→→→→→→→		

Beginning with an Idea

Webster's Dictionary defines idea as *an indefinite or unformed conception* (Merriam-Webster, 2016). When thinking about the concept of an idea in a project-based unit plan, I would apply this definition to the beginning stages of planning. We begin with a blank canvas, an idea. Our starting point allows us to project a path of learning within the framework for planning. We begin with naming a topic around which to build inquiry and discovery.

In the first step of the framework, turn to your state standards, students' interests, or a list of engaging topics to choose and name a topic of learning for the upcoming project. This is where the excitement begins because there are truly endless possibilities for project topics. Let's look into a few ideas for project topics and the thinking behind them.

In my work in supporting groups of teachers in the planning process of fleshing out an entire project unit, one question continues to resonate: "How broad should we go when deciding on a project topic?" This is an important question and brings a key point to the surface. PBL is about each child becoming an expert in some area of the project. The students develop their own expertise as the project progresses and the learners are drawn to an area of interest within the unit topic. So, my answer becomes that a topic can be as broad or as narrow as the teacher thinks the topic can be planned. For example, if a teacher selected a farm as the project topic, there are a multitude of ideas and areas to talk and learn about. This project may last for a few weeks as the children explore and discover the many facets of a farm. Likewise, another teacher may choose to narrow in on the working parts of a farm and plan several unit topics throughout the year, that place an emphasis on the one big idea, a farm. A narrowed approach to teaching the many facets of a farm may be to plan a unit on vegetables, another on machines, and a third on cows. There are many ways to begin thinking about a topic selection when planning the project. Don't be afraid to try on a broad topic and then a narrower topic. You'll see that they each have pros and cons and both offer important ideas to consider when planning.

Below, I've listed just a few ideas to consider in the planning process.

Broad Topics

TABLE 3.2
Broad list of project-based topics for unit creation

Weather	Community Helpers	Habitats	Animals	Cultures	Structures	Explorers
Farms	Simple Machines	Oceans	Transportation	Rocks	Plants	Presidents
The Solar System	Important People	Earth	Insects	Sports		

Narrowed Topics from A to Z

There are endless possibilities of ideas when thinking about a project topic; and exciting ideas waiting to be explored by you and your students. It's a joy to know that project topics can change from year to year as class populations shift and student interests' change.

TABLE 3.3

Narrowed list of project-based topics for unit creation

A	B	C	D	E
Apples	Butterflies	Caterpillars	Dentist	Evergreens
Ants	Bridges	Castles	Dirt	Eating Healthy
Alligators	Bees	Cardboard	Dolphins	Exercise
Authors	Buses	Coral Reefs	Dogs	Earth Day
Astronauts	Boats	Camping	Dinosaurs	Eagles
Abraham	Beavers	Chinese	Dragonflies	Earthquakes
Lincoln	Bicycles	Culture	Design	Erosion
Architecture	Bread	Clouds	Solutions	Electricity
Angles	Bakery	Caves		Emergency
Art	Bugs	Construction		Helpers
Animal Homes	Bears	Vehicles		
Aquarium	Books	Cake		
	Birds	Carpentry		
	Banking	Colors		
	Babies	Coral Reefs		
		Constellations		
		Civil Rights		
		Cats		
		Circuits		

F	G	H	I	J
Fred Rogers	Gardens	Hats	Ice Cream	Jets
Fans	Giraffes	Hair Salon	Igloos	Jellyfish
Fish	Grasshoppers	Hens	Instruments	Johnny
Friends	Grocery Store	Harbors	Inventions	Appleseed
Firefighters	Gravity	Houses	Inventors	Jungle
Frogs		Hummingbirds		
Farming				
Fairy Tales				
Force and				
Motion				
Fruits				
Families				
Feet Types				

K	L	M	N	O
Kindness	Ladybugs	Mail	Neighbors	Orchards
Koalas	Lions	Moon	Newspapers	Owls
Kites	Lizards	Martin Luther	Nests	Omnivores
Kangaroos	Lawnmowers	King, Jr.	Narwhals	Opinions
	Lakes	Mommies	Nursery	
	Leaders	Mud	Rhymes	
		Museums		
		Mythology		

(Continued)

TABLE 3.3 (Continued)

P	Q	R	S	T
Pulley System	Quails	Racecars	Snakes	Tree Houses
Police	Queens	Rockets	Swans	Tornadoes
Pumpkins		Recycle	Sun	Thunderstorms
Planes		Rivers	Swamp	T- Rex
Polar Bears		Rainbows	Sharks	Trains
Post Office		Rabbits	Shoes	Tractors
Playgrounds		Restaurant	Shells	Teeth
Picnics		Robots	Sound	Trees
Pond		Roads	Snow	Toys
Pet Shop		Reindeer	Scientists	Turtles
Parades		Rainforest	Sea Turtles	
Paleontologists		Ramps	Ships	
Pirates		Root Systems	Seasons	
Patterns			Simple	
Poetry			Machines	
Photography			Skyscrapers	
Plumbing			Shadows	
U	V	W	X	Y
Umbrellas	Volcanoes	Water Pipes		
	Vultures	Winter		
	Vegetables	Waves		
		Water Cycle		
		Whales		
		Worms		
		Wolves		
		Wood		
Z				
Zebras				
Zoos				

Entering the Three Phases of Project-Based Learning (PBL)

Phase One

Phase One is an immersion into the learning and topic. In this phase, learners are be introduced to the topic with a focus wall. The focus wall will be created and worked on collaboratively by the students and their teacher. Focus wall work continues throughout the duration of the unit. It includes pictures, information, charts, graphs, student work, student thinking, questions, and anything else that enhances knowledge about the topic that the students uncover or participate in finding.

We'll talk in-depth about the focus wall in Chapter 4. Phase One also includes opportunities for students to pose questions, share prior knowledge and begin to develop an inquiry mindset around the topic.

Both the students and the teacher play important roles throughout Phase One. The teacher gives students opportunities to interact with the topic, immerses them in learning and gains an understanding of what each student already knows about the topic. Each person in the classroom has a shared role in learning, where the students and their teacher are learning alongside each other. Once the topic is presented, deep inquiry, investigation and exploration can begin.

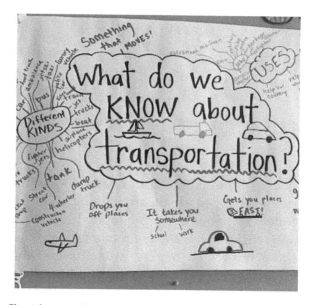

FIGURE 3.1 Chart documenting what learners know about transportation.

Phase One also allows teachers to monitor any misconceptions students may have. This is helpful because it informs the next few days when building and extending content knowledge. Phase One sets students up to learn through lively conversations with classmates, sharing previous knowledge and, most importantly, building curiosity around the project topic.

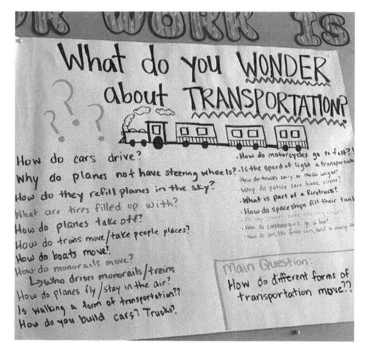

FIGURE 3.2 Chart documenting what learners wonder about transportation.

Questioning plays a key role in Phase One of project-based learning. The teacher can create an ongoing chart full of questions the students wonder about the topic. These questions support and motivate students as they move forward in the project phases. As the project days pass, students are investigating, reading and uncovering answers to the questions they posed. In Chapter 2, we discussed the importance of the teacher dropping the role of sole information giver. Keep this shift at the forefront of your mind during Phase One, because it's easy to fall back into dispersing information to students instead of approaching it through an inquiry mindset in side-by-side learning. Through their inquiry, investigations and discovery, students become motivated to gain their own content knowledge and answer the questions they pondered.

TABLE 3.4

Table highlighting the three phases of project-based learning

Topic Selection Webbing	Phase One	Phase Two	Phase Three
	• Immersion into topic • Focus wall • Collect information • Observe students • Gather information about what students already know • Find out about any misconceptions • Students pose questions/wonders		

Phase Two

In the second phase of PBL, students begin to explore through inquiry and research. As they build their content knowledge and begin developing an area of interest within the topic, students work toward creating a culminating project that displays and explains their expert knowledge. Phase Two is the longest phase of the three phases. There are many things happening in Phase Two, including field trips, whole-group investigations, inquiry stations, and independent research. Students will have a finished project at the end of Phase Two.

In the beginning of Phase Two, the teacher's role is to deepen students understanding around the topic by giving students opportunities to discover, explore, research and appreciate new findings about the topic. The teacher plans relevant field trips (in-person or virtual), creates inquiry stations for exploration and discovery, questions students about their learning journey, highlights new information found by students, observes and records students in their learning and supports students in working toward their culminating projects. Throughout the entire phase, the teacher is constantly questioning students, as whole class, in groups or individually. As you can see, this phase is all about working to harvest a child's natural inclination of wonder and discovery.

Throughout Phase Two, teachers are continually providing opportunities for discovery learning. Field trips provide students with authentic opportunities for observation and discussion. They get to practice field note taking and have the overall experience of being absorbed in the content. Unfortunately, since a large majority of my work in leading the early childhood team was happening in the middle of the pandemic, visiting a site for a field study was definitely not an option. But instead of forfeiting the opportunity for students to have firsthand learning experience, we looked for a new avenue for students. While certainly not replacing the rich experience of visiting a learning site, virtual field trips were the next best learning opportunity. The internet offers a wide variety of talks and ideas on every topic and there are many videos geared to early learners.

While mapping out a unit on transportation during the pandemic, we relied upon out-of-the-box thinking to provide experiences to students. In the early stages of Phase Two, students walked out to the playground where one of the teachers had her car parked with all four doors open and the trunk popped up. Students walked around the car with opportunities to observe, inquire and document their own learning. They talked with classmates about their findings and what they wondered about, as they stood around the teacher's car. Students took notes on their clipboards by drawing their observations and labeling their findings. Although many of them ride in a car every single day, this experience provided a new lens on vehicles, and they loved every minute of it. Another teacher brought in her son's ride-on electronic toy car and displayed it in her classroom for the duration of the project. Offering students an opportunity to observe a transportation model that was just their size. Another teacher on the team wrote to a parent in the classroom who was an airline pilot, asking if he would Zoom with the kindergarteners. This provided learners with an opportunity to learn more about a pilot's responsibility and to ask questions about the profession. Each of these field experiences brought learning to life for the inquisitive kindergarteners. They gained real-life experience in their topic, which then guided them as they developed answers to their questions and deepened their understanding around the project topic. The experiences also heightened their awareness of transportation happening all around them. We noticed that the students couldn't stop talking about transportation! They continuously brought it up in their conversations. Students were constantly thinking and talking about project-related learning. Their worlds were expanding!

Imagine a family loading up into a car and the first words out of the small child's mouth as they buckled in were, "Mommy and daddy, did you know that the car moves forward because it uses a wheel and axle system?" Yes, that is powerful language and thinking coming from a five-year-old, and those are the conversations that project-based learning brings to our learners. They are constantly staying curious about the world around them. Would this conversation have been likely if the learning around transportation involved cut-and-paste worksheets asking students to match the transportation to its name? While there is a time and a place for worksheets in the classroom, but not in project-based learning. We're replacing the worksheet model with hands-on learning experiences, student journaling and project creations.

FIGURE 3.3 A butterfly inquiry station for students to investigate and observe in phase two.

Phase Two also includes inquiry stations that are set up to invite learners to actively seek answers to the questions they posed. As students visit the stations, they are given many opportunities to interact with a lens on a certain area of a topic. Stations invite students to explore things related to the topic, on more in-depth level.

When considering the set-up of an inquiry station, a teacher should include a few materials for discovery. For example, each station should be stocked with books pertaining to that topic focus, pictures for a close-up view, an inquiring question to get them thinking and working and materials to create and discover. Since each station is different and offers the learners with new opportunities, each station must contain different materials. If students are building or creating, they may need blocks, boxes or other construction materials. An art station may include paint, paintbrushes and large sheets of paper to support their artistic visions of bringing the topic to life through paint.

FIGURE 3.4 Student painting a flower in an inquiry station.

In one early childhood project unit, the team and I planned together choosing the topic of flowers. As we thought about the creating inquiry stations, we decided that studying artist Georgia O'Keeffe's flower paintings would be an excellent way to bring in art while students discovered details about flowers up close. Students were excited to see the station and couldn't wait to start painting with purpose. The teachers placed several pictures of Georgia's paintings, some paintbrushes, water, watercolors and flowers on the table. When students first arrived at the inquiry station, they spent time carefully analyzing her flower paintings and compared them to the real version of the flower.

FIGURE 3.5 Students investigating the parts of a flower and painting their discoveries.

Students were invited to create a Georgia O'Keeffe-type masterpiece by bringing an aspect of a flower or flowers to life on paper, using paint as their medium (Georgia O'Keeffe Museum, 2022). The finished products were stunning, and students were able to share information about their flower, such as its type, color, size, shape, where it's found and a lot more. Their pictures became a topic of conversation, as well as documentation of the deep learning in which they were absorbed in.

In another station featuring spider webs, students were invited to carefully look at the shapes and patterns in spider webs. It was set up with pictures of spider webs, books on how spiders spin their webs, glue, tape, white yarn, black construction paper, cardboard squares, and pencils. Students had the opportunity to create spider webs using their prior knowledge about webs and their newly acquired knowledge from the supporting books and photographs in the inquiry station.

FIGURE 3.6 The learner is creating a spider web at an inquiry station.

The goal of every inquiry station is to inspire a deeper understanding of the topic by allowing for organic discovery. Students begin to answer their own questions about the topic as they engage in rich conversations with their fellow classmates while working side by side in the station. Each station offers different learning opportunities ranging from building to observing.

Projects in Phase Two

In the early stages of Phase Two students are expanding their understanding of a topic through books, pictures, conversations, expert talks, field trips and inquiry stations while the teacher is continually observing each student. The teacher looks to see where students show progress and where they may need more support. As a result of these daily observations, the teacher also uncovers what specific area of the project is of most interest to each child. Sometimes this area of interest is obvious, but sometimes the teacher asks specific questions to learn more about a child's interest. As the teacher uncovers each child's area of interest, she can support the child in helping him think about how he would like to demonstrate his area of expertise with the culminating project.

Once the inquiry stations come to a close, the culminating projects begin. Students share their expert knowledge in a focused area of the topic by creating a culminating project. The project results from the deep knowledge gained through research in the topic throughout Phase Two. The great news is that there are no specific guidelines for what the project needs to be or look like. It is entirely up to the child. Students that share the same expert interest may want to put their ideas together and work as a team or in partners. Projects can be done individually, in pairs, in groups, and, sometimes, might wind up being a whole class project.

In the end of Phase Two, students work on their projects over the course of a few days. They research, read, converse, and create. As students busily work, it's interesting for the teacher to watch how their final projects unfold. Each project looks different from the rest. Students have the ability to let their creative side guide the project. They use a variety of mediums to create projects and display expert knowledge. In the next chapter, we'll carefully look at project ideas and media for creation.

In the project creation portion of Phase Two the teacher's role is to support the learner as they work to demonstrate and display their content knowledge. The student has taken on the role of lead learner. As support, teachers can offer books for reading, provide creation materials, hold extended conversations about the student's area of expertise and serve as a thought partner in the project creation. The beauty of projects is that every child is creating something unique that highlights their own expert knowledge gained in this topic focus.

FIGURE 3.7 Examples of culminating projects that display expert knowledge.

One quick glance at these pictures reveals an open window into the wide world of project creation. Both pictures highlight a different medium used to display expert knowledge.

Pictured at the top is the Terracotta Army from China. Two preK-4 students showed a particular interest in learning more about the first emperor of China's grand mausoleum. They created figures from playdough to support their findings.

Other students worked to display their expertise in a jungle habitat. They used building blocks, paper, playdough, animal figurines, markers, tape and glue to bring his habitat to life. Students worked in a group of four to create their final project. As Phase Two progressed, the teacher noted that all four of these students showed an interest in learning more about jungles.

Each project is different and unique. They display the learners' deeper understanding of content knowledge and their approach of displaying their new expertise through a model.

TABLE 3.5

Table highlighting the second of the three phases of project-based learning

Topic Selection Webbing	Phase One	Phase Two	Phase Three
	• Immersion into topic • Focus Wall • Collect information • Observe students • Gather information about what students already know • Find out about any misconceptions • Students pose questions/wonders	• In-person or virtual field trips • Investigations • Focus wall additions • Expert talks • Field guides • Dramatic play • Inquiry stations • Projects launch • Projects completed	

Concluding with Phase Three

After days and weeks of exciting learning centered around one specific topic, students are ready to share their learned knowledge with others. The culminating projects have already been completed in Phase Two, and it's time to move into presenting the final projects. The final step of concluding this large project is to give students the opportunity to present their gained expert knowledge with others.

Students spend a day planning presentations and considering who they might like to invite to learn more about their topic of focus. There are a variety of ways to consider sharing the knowledge with others in the school and the surrounding community.

Once decided, the celebratory planning may begin. Often students like to share their learning with their parents and students in the school. They may decide to invite neighboring classes to the presentations, or the teacher might record the project presentations and send them out in a movie to all the parents. In some instances, parents come to the presentation day. Each project's audience for celebration day can vary. Each project's audience for celebration day can vary depending on the invited guests. It may include participants ranging from parents and visiting classes to administration and enrichment teachers.

If in-person guests are not an option, a video camera capturing the joy in learning is a great option. Throughout the year as projects conclude, the presentation day offers students with experience in presenting to an audience and enhancing their speaking and listening skills.

Presenting projects gives students the opportunity to share what they've learned about the project topic with others. Each child offers new insights on the project and a glimpse into their specific interest. One by one, the student, partner pair or group stands up to present their model and expert knowledge. At the end of each presentation, the audience or other classmates can ask questions of the expert.

As the project comes to a close, students will have had the opportunity to fully engage in discovery, inquiry, research, conversation, documentation, and creation around a central topic. Once this style of learning is introduced to our young learners, they develop the natural inclination to be intrinsically motivated to find out more about topics through discovery. They begin participating in this type of learning no matter where they are and what they may be doing. Project-based learning employs the highest levels of thinking and learning on Bloom's Taxonomy (McDaniel 2022).

The three phases in PBL take the learner from the lowest level of Bloom's, to the highest level, creation, where learners are investigating, designing and developing a model to share their learning.

TABLE 3.6

Table highlighting the final phase in project-based learning

Topic Selection Webbing	Phase One	Phase Two	Phase Three
	• Immersion into topic • Focus wall • Collect information • Observe students • Gather information about what students already know • Find out about any misconceptions • Students pose questions/wonders	• In-person or virtual field trips • Investigations • Focus wall additions • Expert talks • Field guides • Dramatic play • Inquiry stations • Projects launched • Projects completed	• Celebrate with project presentations • Plan the project celebration • Display of final projects • Answer all student posed questions

Planning a Timeline

I have often been asked how long each of the three phases should last. Sometimes as teachers it's easy to plan things in periods of weeks. For example, Phase One lasts for one week, Phase Two lasts for one week and Phase Three lasts for a week, leaving this as a three-week project. Remember earlier in this chapter we talked about dropping the stringent rules on planning a PBL unit? A teacher should consider that same idea when planning a timeline for the unit. We don't need to get stuck in week timespans. Each PBL unit contains different opportunities for learning, different project ideas and a different approach to discovering more about the topic, which leads us to conclude that each project will have a different timeline. While some projects may last for three to four weeks, others may be short one-week projects, depending on the topic and student interest throughout the project. As we move through the three phases, let's consider the ideas we want to develop or discover and the time it will take to do that, instead of thinking in terms of weeks. Each PBL unit will have a different timeline.

For example, in a preK-3 classroom, the teachers and I wrote a ten-day PBL unit on ice cream. It involved creating a dramatic play ice cream parlor, making ice cream, understanding where ice cream comes from and many other learning opportunities. In the same classroom we wrote a PBL unit on oceans in which it lasted 14 days. We included many facets of the ocean which extended the inquiry and timeline.

In beginning the planning process, think in terms of content, depth and activities instead of weeks. Ask yourself these questions:

1. How long will we spend getting to know the topic?
2. Will students create individual projects, or will we create a class project?
3. Does this project include field trips?
4. What areas of the topic will we explore?
5. Am I including math and reading standards?

These are some guiding questions that will help to determine the timeline of a project. Be comfortable knowing that each project has its own agenda, timeline and opportunities for discovery.

Chapter 3 Reflection

What PBL topics are you considering?

Are you planning this unit independently or with your grade-level team? What might be important to consider in making sure all voices are heard in the planning process?

Dramatic Play – Learning from the Childlike Mindset

FIGURE 3.8 This child is setting up a snowball stand and highlighting the childlike mindset in learning through play.

What is the learning taking place while setting up a snowball stand or any dramatic play area?

How is this learning transferring to into real life experiences?

What are the visible levels of Bloom's Taxonomy being applied in dramatic play?

References

Georgia O'Keeffe Museum. (2022, March 7). *About Georgia O'Keeffe – The.* https://www.okeeffemuseum.org/about-georgia-okeeffe/

McDaniel, R. (2022, June 10). *Bloom's Taxonomy.* Vanderbilt University. https://cft.vanderbilt.edu/guides-sub-pages/blooms-taxonomy/

Merriam-Webster. (2016). *The Merriam-Webster Dictionary, Mass-Market Paperback* (Newest ed.). Merriam-Webster, Inc.

4

The Planning Process

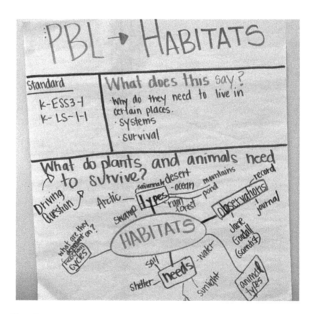

FIGURE 4.1 The planning process beginning with a topic web.

Thoughts and ideas come together to support an overall learning goal at the beginning of a project. Albert Einstein offers these wise words: "If I had an hour to solve a problem, I would spend the first fifty-five minutes determining the proper question to ask, for once I know the proper question, I could solve the problem in less than five minutes." (The Build Network, 2021).

DOI: 10.4324/9781003332541-4

A few essential questions to consider as we embark on project-based unit teaching are:

1. What is it that we want our learners to walk away knowing after each unit?
2. How will we measure success and mastery of standards?
3. What will continue to drive the learning and unit forward?

We can embrace Einstein's words as we consider these questions. The learning goal is determined once these questions are answered. Our learning goal will set the course or path to support the planning process.

Chapter 4 provides a variety of ideas to support the planning process. We will go through each phase once more; this time, however, we'll put a lens over actual structures and activities you may consider including in your plans. This chapter aims to create a toolbox of strategies in each phase to set you up for success in planning a project-based unit.

Topic Webbing – Choosing and Thinking on Paper

In its simplest form, topic webbing supports the teacher in thinking about almost every aspect of the topic. It's simply a tool to get you started with the planning process. Once you've selected your topic, the webbing helps you consider your options around the content. The example image below shows the project topic in the center of the web, and the bubbles around it show as many things to know about the topic that can be studied. The smaller bubbles are considered subtopics or highlighted areas. Whether you're planning with your grade-level team or on your own, webbing is your second step after choosing a topic in the planning process. You may consider webbing on a blank sheet of paper or even large chart paper. The beauty of webbing is that it can be messy because thinking and planning are messy, but a good messy!

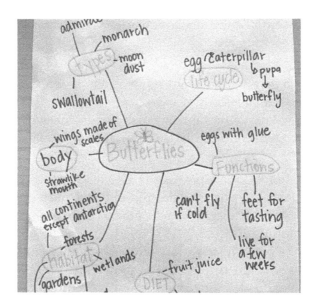

FIGURE 4.2 Example of topic webbing.

Naming the Driving Question

At the beginning of this chapter, we posed three questions to consider when planning a project-based unit. The third question, "What will continue to drive the learning and unit forward?," is essential to the overall unit plan. At the beginning of Phase One, the driving question helps students and remains visible in conversation and research throughout the entire unit. While learners are working toward answering their questions about the topic, they are working toward the ability to answer that one driving question. By the end of the unit, students should have gained enough knowledge to participate in an active conversation around the driving question, providing many examples and supporting the answer to the driving question with facts from their research.

Naming the driving question helps the learner use their knowledge to answer the question in various ways. In other words, the question should remain open, leaving behind a simple one-word answer.

TABLE 4.1

Examples of possible project topics with driving questions

Project-Based Unit Topic	Driving Question
Transportation	What is important about transportation?
Flowers	What makes flowers special?
Simple Machines	How are simple machines helpful?
Oceans	Why are oceans important?
Habitats	What do plants and animals need to survive?

Aligning to the Standards

Each state, school, daycare, and homeschooling program has set guidelines about what students should master as they progress through school. Frequently, they are referred to as state standards and can be found on any state Department of Education website. These standards set goals for students in each grade level and frequently begin at infancy and move up through high school. It's best to align your units to a set of standards. It supports the learners as they progress through the year while holding the teacher accountable for including and teaching specific focuses in each content area. Standards may include math goals, literacy goals, speaking and listening goals, science goals, social studies goals, etc. When linking standards to your project unit, it is good to keep a running list or highlight what you've already taught this year. It helps you stay focused on making sure to introduce every single standard and revisit specific standards throughout the school year.

Planning Phase One

While planning for Phase One, it's important to keep in mind the goals of the first phase.

Phase One Goals:

◆ Introduce the learners to the topic
◆ Immerse learners in topic content organically

- ◆ Begin the development of the focus wall
- ◆ Provide opportunities for the learners to ask questions about the topic
- ◆ Discover what students already know about the topic
- ◆ Uncover any misconceptions students may have about the topic

What might this look like in your learning space or classroom? No matter who enters your learning space, whether it's a student, director, or colleague, it should be evident what your topic of discovery is for your unit. The visual unfolding of the learning begins throughout Phase One, and the wall space will start to include evidence of learning as the unit progresses. Students should see their thinking and learning all over the classroom.

As the planning process begins for the learning progression in Phase One, let's consider a few ideas. Since there is no timeline for Phase One, the crucial things to consider when thinking about time are:

- ◆ What should be appreciated and valued in introducing the topic to my learners?
- ◆ How can I unfold this topic organically and encourage high curiosity levels in my young learners?

Lens Over Phase One – A Toolbox of Strategies and Ideas

A Book Display – A collection of books full of inquisitive potential just waiting for eager readers to unlock is a staple in the project's early days. A great way to develop an interest in a topic and share the potential possibilities for learning is a large display of books focused on the topic of discovery. Where might you gather a collection of books on any topic? You may consider visiting the public library, school library, or your collection of books, or consider purchasing a few each year to add to the unit. I love going to garage sales now to find many bargains on books!

The Focus Wall – The focus wall is a compilation of learning, information, and documentation of the unit. On the opening day of the project unit, the focus wall is usually the first place to begin. The focus wall should be in a central location in your classroom, where students can continuously interact with the learning.

What does the focus wall contain?

- ◆ Photographs of the topic of study
- ◆ Charts, graphs and thinking maps created with students
- ◆ A class-generated list of questions
- ◆ Organically evolved vocabulary words and their student-friendly drawings of the definition
- ◆ Drawings, diagrams or paintings from the students
- ◆ Information uncovered about the topic of study
- ◆ Anything that supports students in their discovery of the topic

FIGURE 4.3 Example of project focus wall.

A focus wall is a central piece of the project. It's a place where many new ideas and thoughts are collected and displayed.

Students begin to take ownership of their learning when they interact with the learning on the focus wall. It becomes a place of reference and documentation of learning. The focus wall begins on the first day of the unit and should be continually revisited to add new ideas. It is a work in progress for the duration of the unit. Both students and teacher are frequently adding to the wall.

Photographs – Photographs are a vital resource in each phase. Photographs give the learner a real glimpse of the topic up close. They invite learners to observe patterns, details, and information about the topic. Collect your pictures in various ways: the internet, websites for photograph collections, or your own collection. Once you find photographs, you can send them to a local photo developer or print them from a printer. It is a good idea to laminate the photographs so they remain in good condition and withstand many inquisitive fingers and eyes.

How can photographs/pictures be utilized throughout the unit?

◆ They can be placed around the room as a gallery walk, where students can observe the topic and engage in conversations with classmates.
◆ They can hang on the focus wall for the duration of the unit.
◆ They can be placed in inquiry stations in Phase Two.
◆ They can be used as a conversational piece in whole-group discussions.

Exploration Instruments – Exploration instruments are a great way to immerse learners in the content and topic. Invite students to sit in a circle with the tools/instruments in the center. Give students time to explore the objects and talk with classmates about what they notice. You should create a list of your observations from what is shared during the exploration. As the students share ideas while exploring, the teacher can document their ideas on chart paper. Then, the documented observation chart can be added to the focus wall.

Example: Suppose a prek-4 class is beginning a unit on gardening. The teacher places shovels, watering cans, empty pots, gloves, a small wheelbarrow, and any other gardening tools she has on hand in the center of the circle. She invites students to observe and touch the gardening tools and talk with friends in the circle about what they notice or know. The teacher is listening in on conversations and observing student actions. While students are conversing, the teacher records ideas from the students on the chart paper. After a few minutes of exploration, the class comes back together, and the teacher shares the thoughts from the chart and adds additional ideas to the chart.

Read-alouds – Beginning each day with a read-aloud is the perfect way to introduce new content knowledge and support students as they make connections with prior knowledge or new ideas. During read-alouds, the teacher reads a text aloud to the students while stopping periodically throughout the text to invite students to converse about the content. Consider seating students in a circle or square around the rug in your classroom as you read aloud to them. Seating students in a way that mimics the dinner table, moving away from traditional rows, cultivates the opportunity for more substantial conversations. While the teacher is reading aloud from a book that supports the topic, she will stop a few times during the book reading to ask questions or consider an idea that was just read. During pauses, students can talk with partners or as a whole class. The circle seating arrangement invites all students to be mentally present, making eye contact with the speaker and considering new ideas presented in the conversation. These meaningful daily conversations support students as they begin to make meaning of the text and link new ideas to the topic of study. A read-aloud is usually the opener to each day in Phase One, supporting the student in learning more about the topic and making connections.

Charts and Thinking Maps – Charts and thinking maps are a fantastic way to categorize information learned and record new ideas. Interactive charts offer students the ability to see ideas about the topic come together. There are a variety of charts and graphs that can be brought into Phase One. Once the teacher and students create the chart together, it can hang on the focus wall for the duration of the unit. Students will visit the focus wall throughout the day, as they begin to make meaning of the topic. Placing the visible ideas together with their thinking and a thinking map gives them an ample opportunity to revisit learning repeatedly. The focus wall will continually grow with informational content as the learners gain new knowledge.

TABLE 4.2
Table displaying various types of thinking maps

Types of Charts and Thinking Maps

Circle Map

A circle map places the topic in the center and invites learners to share all they know and are learning.

Tree Map

A tree map allows learners to classify information already known and learned throughout the unit.

(Continued)

TABLE 4.2 (Continued)

Types of Charts and Thinking Maps

Bubble Map	A bubble map creates opportunities for students to describe a topic and its many features.

ABC Chart	An ABC chart is an amazing way to chart and track new information categorized by the letters in the alphabet.

Make-Believe and Short Skits – Often, the topic of study lends itself to a skit, demonstration, or some type of play. This is a wonderful opportunity for students to fully immerse themselves in bringing the learning to life.

A few examples of PBL topics of study include:

Birds – The teacher might invite students to practice the up and down motion of birds' wings when flying and the V formation that birds often create in the air.

Emergency Helpers – Students might put on a skit of firefighters leaving the firehouse, driving to a fire and pretending to put the fire out.

Construction Vehicles – Students might act as different construction vehicles as they learn about the different jobs of
each vehicle.

Drawings – Quick sketches or intricate drawings are an excellent addition to the project's early days in Phase One. As the
student draws his knowledge of the topic, the teacher can
gain a glimpse of his thought processes. Drawings support
the teacher's understanding of what the child is interested
in, their knowledge of the topic, and even their misunder-
standings. At the beginning of a project unit on transportation, a kindergarten teacher asked her students to draw
a picture of a mode of transportation. In this image, it's
apparent that the child is quite knowledgeable about buses,
a school bus in particular. A glimpse at this drawing would
help the teacher support this learner as they build on current
knowledge and nurture a deeper understanding of different types of transportation and even other buses and their
different uses. A quick conversation with this child about
this drawing would also unveil a few wonders. Does the
child know about other types of buses? What is the primary
purpose of a bus? After the drawings are complete, students
visit the focus wall for all to enjoy, ponder and converse.

FIGURE 4.4 Drawing to gain insight on student's understanding of content.

Questions and Wonders – As the project kicks off, students will begin to develop a list of questions and what they wonder about the topic. During Phase One, it's a good idea for the whole class to begin generating a list of questions about the topic. On large chart paper will be an ongoing list that is revisited daily throughout the unit. As students read, inquire and discover, they find answers to the questions posed on the chart. The answers to the questions can be posted on the chart next to each question. This wonder chart allows students to truly take on the role of the researcher as they find answers to their questions.

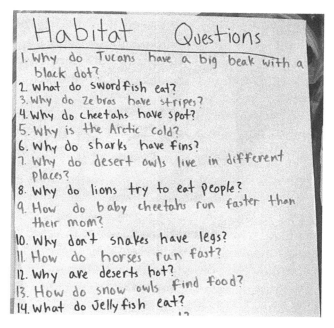

FIGURE 4.5 List of student wonders posed in Phase One.

Project Message Writing – Project messages are a perfect way to highlight new information, ask wonder questions, and involve learners in the writing process. Project messages are usually one of the first parts of each day during Phase One.

These are messages the teacher writes to her students that bring aspects of the project to light by reminiscing about a previous day's learning, posing wonder questions, and inviting students to interact with the text printed on the message. The messages are usually written on large chart paper before beginning learning that day. There are a wide variety of ways to create daily messages.

During the day's message, students gather in a central meeting space, usually the carpet area, to read, converse and add to the message. A project message consists of a few different parts that invite students to interact with the topic different ways.

1. Messages often begin with a review of the learning from previous days or peek into that day's focus.
2. Messages offer an opportunity for students to pon- der a question and answer it as an interactive writing exercise.
3. Messages support students as they connect ideas about the topic together.

Interactive writings are a way for students to engage in the writing process alongside the teacher. The entire class takes part in the construction of the text or message. Stan Swartz (2001) introduced the concept of interactive writing as "a teaching method in which children and teacher negoti- ate what they are going to write and then share the pen to construct the message." During this part of the message, the students support the teacher in sharing ideas to write on the message paper, while the teacher may invite a few students to help construct the text by using "sharing the pen." After each project message is complete, the message poster hangs near the focus wall as an added piece of research and dis- covery. The students will continue to interact with the proj- ect message as it hangs on the wall. Throughout the day, students continuously make meaning from the constructed text, pictures, and message, by revisiting the learning that happened during that moment.

FIGURE 4.6 Sample project message which can be used during Phases One and Two.

Planning Phase Two

While planning for Phase Two, it's important to continuously keep in mind the goals of the second phase.

Phase Two Goals:

◆ Provide students with opportunities to deepen their content knowledge through investigations and conversations

◆ Design opportunities for real-world experiences through field trips or virtual field trips

◆ Create multiple opportunities for discovery

◆ Observe students in their work and thinking

◆ Record daily observations of students and their findings, interests and discoveries

◆ Set up a variety of inquiry stations where students have opportunities to expand their knowledge on the topic

◆ Facilitate learning through questioning

◆ Create and construct final projects based on the students' interests

◆ Record answers to the questions they pose and converse openly about them

Remember, Phase Two is the longest of the three phases and the most intricate. It involves many opportunities for discovery, conversation, and observation. What does the learning in Phase Two look like in your learning space? Since Phase One has come to a close, the learning space is already filled with excellent information about the topic of study. It is displayed all over the learning space through the focus wall, student drawings, project messages, book displays, and other forms of learning. Our job in Phase Two is to bring the learning to life through discovery experiences for our students. They will participate in research through field studies and expert talks, visit inquiry stations, make meaning with their newly gained knowledge, develop a specific expertise area, and create a project to share their specialist knowledge.

As the planning process continues with Phase Two, we'll continue to fill our toolbox full of ideas that we may consider including in the second phase of the learning progression. Phase Two is the longest of the three phases.

The important things to consider when thinking about our timeline are:

◆ How will I facilitate learning and provide ample opportunities for discovery and inquiry?
◆ What areas of the topic are my learners interested in and how will I support expansion of their knowledge?
◆ What will the final project involve?
◆ Will we complete a class project together, where students will create different pieces which we'll put together as a whole or will we do group or individual projects?

When considering the beginning of Phase Two which includes student discovery and inquiry stations, it can be arranged in two different ways.

Arrangement #1: Break the days into two parts, beginning with whole-group learning or discovery, and then moving into inquiry stations. Both types of learning happen in the same day. Inquiry station activities typically last for a few days, as one group of students visit one station per day and rotate through each station over many days. As the station rotations come to a close, students are usually ready to begin their expert projects and share their gained knowledge about the topic of study.

Arrangement #2: Separate field study visit and whole-class investigation days from inquiry days. After consecutive days of field studies and investigations, plan for a few consecutive days of rotating through a few inquiry stations.

Both arrangements work well, depending on the PBL topic of study. Feel confident in trying them both as you plan for your upcoming PBL units.

Lens Over Phase Two – A Toolbox of Strategies and Ideas

Field Studies – Field studies bring learning to life and can be done in many ways. In a field study, students participate in an up-close investigation of the topic. Field studies can occur at an actual site off campus or right there in your learning space through a virtual field trip. Whether it's visiting an apple orchard, walking the aisles of a school bus, or talking virtually with an oceanographer, students interact with learning in a real-life experience. Students take notes through drawings during field studies as they uncover new knowledge or validate general knowledge.

Throughout the beginning days of Phase Two, students can participate in a few field studies through various approaches. You may plan for a field trip on the first day, then take virtual field trips and speak with experts in the days following. Consider investing in clipboards to support students in writing down or drawing the expert knowledge they discover. In a project study of simple machines, a preK-4 class walked across the street to the city playground to analyze the use of simple machines at work on the playground. Students watched an expert talk about a specific simple machine and how it operates in the days following.

These experiences provided students with an opportunity to interact with the topic of study. This part of Phase Two is an example of making SHIFT TWO, "dropping the control", and SHIFT FOUR, "you're not the only expert in the room" that we read about in Chapter 2. Instead of the teacher giving students all the information about a topic through field studies, the students themselves gain expert knowledge through hands-on experiences.

Whole-Class Investigations – In a whole-class investigation, students work together with their teacher to solve a problem, strengthen understanding or investigate a new topic area. In whole-class investigations, the teacher introduces a zoomed-in focus of the topic of study and provides materials for students to carry out investigations. The investigations can range from using blocks for building to creating a large class mural. The whole-class investigations usually occur before groups begin moving into inquiry stations. This is a time for learners to work together as a large group, converse about the topic, research together, and connect with their learning. A few examples of whole-class investigations include:

1. In a unit on bears, a preK-3 class read about bears hibernating in the winter. The teacher had materials on hand: a sheet, leaves, flashlights, and construction paper. She asked the students how they might make a bear cave, and for each to take a turn pretending to hibernate in the cave. The students worked together to create a cave by placing the sheet halfway across a table, made signs that said "Bear cave" and "Hibernating bears," and placed leaves on the floor. Each child took a turn using the flashlight to examine the bear cave and compare it to bear cave photographs.

2. In a unit on flowers, students in a preK-4 classroom first looked at different flower types in books and pictures, then took a virtual field trip to a flower garden. The teacher had on hand a large piece of white bulletin board paper, markers, crayons, and paint available for students to use. She asked students to create a garden

mural together by each adding a few things to the sheet of paper. Students first conversed about what they would add to the mural, then began working on their class mural creation. The mural hung outside of their classroom for the entire school to view.

FIGURE 4.7 Garden mural painted by students to display their knowledge of flowers.

3. In a unit on spiders, students analyzed the different types of spiders by looking at photographs in partner pairs. As they observed with magnifying glasses, students recorded their findings in a field guide by drawing pictures of the different types of spiders to document their learning. When the observations were complete, students came together as a whole class to talk about their findings, the teacher wrote their observations on large chart paper and hung it next to the focus wall.

Dramatic Play – Dramatic play is a fantastic way to extend the short skits from Phase One into an actual drama scene, including props, labeled materials, improvised lines, and furniture movement. Dramatic play requires students to make meaning of their learning by applying all their knowledge of the topic through role play. For example, if a class is learning more about pets, they may take time one day during Phase Two to set up a pet shop. After reading about pet shops, looking at photographs, and taking a real or virtual field trip to a pet shop, the class is ready to create their own. Students can decide how the pet shop should be set up, what materials they need, and what jobs each person will have in setting up the dramatic play. Once the plan has been set, students begin his work in setting up. Each student has the opportunity to bring their expert knowledge and ideas into the dramatic play scene, and students need to see that all their opinions are valued. After the dramatic play area is ready, students can spend time role playing in their new creation, giving them ample opportunity to apply their knowledge and try it on in play.

Inquiry Stations – Inquiry stations are a perfect way for students to research, discover, wonder, find answers to their questions and develop expert knowledge. The stations are completely hands-on and one of the highlights of Phase Two. When planning stations to support your project topic, consider the following:

   ◆ Areas of the project students are interested in
   ◆ An opportunity to clear up misconceptions about the topic
   ◆ An opportunity to emphasize a specific area of the topic

After selecting inquiry stations, it's time to gather supplies and develop wonder questions for students to investigate. Each inquiry station is stocked with a few staples, no matter the posed investigation. Stations should include real photographs supporting the area of focus, books for discovery, and various materials for creating and doing. Stations are most often a hands-on discovery without a worksheet or packet. The supporting paper(s) found in the inquiry station is an opportunity for students to show their knowledge by drawing or painting. Supporting papers often include a headline with a blank page following for drawings or observations.

When students visit the inquiry station, it's important to have a station guide, including a wonder question to support their purpose for discovery. The figure below shows that the teacher designed the station around building a deeper understanding of different types of bird beaks. The station title and wonder question are posted with an illustration to pique interests and serve as a support for any nonreaders. Notice that the questions allow students to investigate, observe, and create. There are no step-by-step directions that will end up with each student's outcome as the same product. It's essential to allow students to bring their ideas and creativity to the stations. There are also a variety of photographs illustrating different types of bird beaks and books to share knowledge about the topic. Students are provided with an assortment of materials for building and creating, along with a research page for students to document their knowledge of bird beaks through drawings. This station is set up for students to converse while deepening their understanding and learning about different bird beaks and their purposes.

FIGURE 4.8 Inquiry station where students can discover more about the beaks of birds.

There are many station ideas and support materials that can be incorporated into inquiry stations. The following table puts a lens over example inquiry stations, the wonder question posed, the focus of the station, and materials needed for exploration. These are just a few examples to help spark your ideas for creating inquiry stations in your project unit and by no means the only ideas for inquiry stations. There is an infinite amount of possibilities for station creations.

TABLE 4.3

Sample inquiry station ideas that invite discovery and wonder in project topics

Project Topic and Station Idea	Wonder Question(s)	Focus of Station	Materials Needed
Project Topic-Spiders Station Focus-Spider Eyes	1. What do you notice about a spider's eyes? 2. Create a spider and show what you've learned about their eyes.	The goal of this station is for students to develop a deeper understanding of a spider's eyes, uses, amounts and what they look like. They will reach this goal through deepening their understanding with books, photographs and a model creation of spider eyes.	✍ close-up photographs of spider eyes - supporting books - googly eyes - glue - pipe cleaners - a blank spider body cut out ✍ black pom poms
Project Topic-Farming Station Focus-Farm Sensory Bin	1. What are the spaces of a farm? 2. Where do the animals live? 3. What grows on a farm?	The goal of this station is for students to put all their learning about the farm into working play. They will reach this goal through building and creating a farm scene, then playing with the animals and farm areas. This station will encourage students to apply their learning, use content vocabulary in their conversations and bring their learning to life.	✍ farm animal figurines - farm pictures and books - box for creating a barn - brown construction paper for a mud area - green felt for grass/crops ✍ legos to create animal homes/fences

TABLE 4.3 (Continued)

Project Topic and Station Idea	Wonder Question(s)	Focus of Station	Materials Needed
Project Topic- Pets Station Focus- Pet Washing Station	How do we care for pets and keep them clean?	The goal of this station is for students to extend their dramatic play by focusing in on a specific area of the topic. Students will use given materials to create dramatic play area and pretend through play. They will reach this goal by collaborating to set up and carry out the play.	✍ stuffed animal pets - pet washing pictures - plain paper for sign creation ✍ bottles for play
Project Topic-Ocean Station Focus- Shell Discovery	What do you notice about these shells? Can you draw what you see?	The goal of this station is for students to study shells and their patterns up close. Students will reach this goal as they interact with the real seashells, notice patterns and try to mimic them through drawings.	✍ Pictures of seashells - Real seashells - Magnifying glasses ✍ Drawing paper

During inquiry station time, the teacher's role is to question, observe, and document the learning progressions of each student in the classroom. Taking on the facilitator role during inquiry stations, the teacher discovers more about his/her students, while assisting the advancement of their knowledge and understanding through probing questioning.

Revisiting the Focus Wall

As the learning in the unit concludes in Phase Two, it's always a good idea to revisit the focus wall. A revisit provides the opportunity to conclude the learning by answering lingering questions, reviewing findings, and celebrating all the fantastic learning on and around the focus wall. Students talk about the interesting things they've discovered through a circle time conversation while using the focus wall for discussion and talking points.

Moving Into Projects

At the end of Phase Two, the culminating project displays a student's expert knowledge and demonstrates the learning from each unit. There are a variety of ways to plan a culminating project. The key in planning a successful culminating project is to remember the driving question from the beginning of the unit and evaluate how learners best express expert knowledge about this driving question through the project's creation.

Culminating projects can be done by the whole class, a group, pairs, or an individual. However, the culminating project is decided upon, students are creating something that shares and displays their expert knowledge in a field.

How do you know what the student will want to share and create?

Students tend to favor a specific area as a project develops. As the teacher observes, documents, questions, and discusses throughout the entire unit, she is also helping the student develop their area of expertise within the project. This begins when a child reads a lot on a specific area, talks about it continuously with peers, and researches to answer questions. As the inquiry stations end, the teacher starts talking with students about their final project.

The teacher may ask the students questions like:

◆ What do you think you've become an expert in?
◆ How do you want to share what you're learning with others?
◆ What could you make to share your expert knowledge?

◆ Do you want to create this by yourself, or I've noticed that _____ is an expert in the same area? Would you want to work with him/her?

Below you'll find project ideas for both whole-group projects and individual/group projects. Most importantly, the teacher must offer students a wide variety of options and opportunities to demonstrate their expert knowledge.

Whole-Group Project Ideas

A Mural – A mural is a perfect way for students to create a large and eye-popping piece that contains intricate details about the PBL topic of study. The class designs the mural and the information they'll want to include, then students work independently on parts of the mural. Finally, all the parts come together to make one large piece of work. Consider including labels or informational blurbs explaining more about the topic. Though a mural was also introduced as a whole-class investigation earlier in Phase Two, it can also be a final project if it was not completed earlier in the project.

Museum – Build a museum, where each child works independently on a specific piece or exhibit for the museum. All the pieces then come together to create a class museum showcasing each student's creation, all on the same topic. This creates a marvelous opportunity for sharing knowledge as they work toward one common goal.

Class Play – Students apply their knowledge by putting on a class play about the PBL topic focus and the new information gained. Students are responsible for writing the script, making the costumes and props and designing the set.

A Class Book – Creating a class book is another way great way to put all of our students' expert knowledge together. Students each create a drawing or page of the book that focuses on their specific interest or fact. The teacher complies the pages, and, as she reads aloud, students share even more on their specific page.

Individual, Group or Partner Pair Project Ideas

TABLE 4.4

Table representing culminating project ideas and examples

Project Medium	More on Materials	A Real-Life Example
Book	Stapled sheets of paper come to life as students illustrate and attempt to label or write their expert knowledge.	In a project unit on spiders, one student became particularly interested in Wolf Spiders. He wrote an entire book on a Wolf Spider for his final project.
Drawing	Colored pencils, crayons and markers provide the perfect inspiration for students to create a masterpiece so show and share their expert knowledge.	In a project unit on ants, one child used markers and colored pencils to draw an ant colony complete with chambers for food and many tunnels. She told about the queen's job and the other jobs in the ant colony.
Painting	Watercolor or washable paint bring a facet of the project to life and allows students the opportunity to tap into their artist talents.	A PreK3 class was studying the ocean. Many students painted animals that call the ocean home for their final projects.
Model	Creating a model is one of the most popular options of expert knowledge representation. There are many possibilities which fall under a model creation and allow students the opportunity to build their expert knowledge with different materials. Paper, cardboard, blocks, playdough and loose parts are just a few of the many inspiring materials students can use to build.	1. After studying transportation in a kindergarten classroom, students were working in groups or on their own to begin their project design and creation. One group of four students were specifically interested in cars. They spent about two days using many cardboard boxes to design and create a life size model of a car. In their presentation, they talked about the motor, the working parts and what they included in their build. 2. After studying a unit on the Chinese Culture, PreK4 students were busy creating their model representations of expert knowledge. One student was interested in the Great Wall of China and designed and built a model with glue and sugar cubes. When he presented it to the class, he shared his knowledge of it while he pointed out specific parts on his model.

Stop Motion Video	In an effort to bring in aspects of technology to the classroom, stop motion videos are an amazing way to bring topics to life. There are a variety of stop motion Apps that can be downloaded to a phone or iPad and are user friendly for our littles.	In a project unit on important people, two students chose to create a stop motion video on Maya Angelou. They included figures, drawings and sayings of Maya Angelou.
Puppet	Bringing characters, places or animals to life through puppetry is a perfect way for learners to share more about their expert knowledge.	In a project unit on dogs, a sock puppet was designed and created with markers, paper and buttons.
Play	Acting out expert knowledge is a wonderful way for learners to apply their newly gained expertise.	In a project unit on the Solar System, groups of kindergarten students created different models of the planets and then acted out their final presentation using their planet props. They shared newly gained expert knowledge about their planet.
Song	Writing a song is a perfect way to apply the learned knowledge into rhythm and beats.	In a unit on picnics, a child decided to take a known song and rewrite the words. She wrote about a perfect picnic party telling what items were needed, who was invited and the planned activities at the picnic.

In preparation for the creation of many projects happening all at once, it's important to have supplies ready and on hand for students to use as they create. Often, students know where supplies are located in the classroom and can access them when needed. After each child has decided on the medium in which they will showcase their expert knowledge, they can begin their masterpieces.

Once the project creations are complete, the focus wall has been finalized and most questions have been answered, it's time to move into the final phase of the project, Phase Three. As Phase Two comes to a close, the learning will still progress, even into Phase Three. In Phase Three, students have the opportunity to learn from their classmates during their presentations of expert knowledge on the celebration day!

Lens Over Phase Three – A Toolbox of Strategies and Ideas

While planning for Phase Three, keep in mind the goals of the last phase of the project.

Phase Three Goals:

◆ Provide students with opportunities to share their expert knowledge through presentations
◆ Finalize any documentation of either student work to be displayed or teacher observation notes
◆ Open your learning space by inviting outside guests (administration, faculty, parents, other classes) to hear presentations from students

Phase Three is usually the shortest of the three phases. It can be thought of as a celebration of learning phase. In the beginning of Phase Three, students decide who they would like to invite to their presentation day. After establishing their audience, students get to work creating invitations, a stage or any other needed items for the presentation day.

Working Up to Presentation Day

In the initial days of Phase Three, students spend time preparing for the presentation day. On this day, students will present their final projects and share their expert knowledge with an audience. The work before this day involves students designing and making invitations and creating the presentation area. Invitations are made with paper and markers or videoed to be emailed out to guests. However, the class decides to create the invitation; it's up to the students to design, create and send out before the big presentation day.

Once invitations have been sent out, the lineup of presentations should be decided upon with the help of the students. A few things to take into consideration when creating the lineup of presentations.

◆ Are there any models or sets that need to be set up ahead of time?

These might be considered for the first round of presentations.
◆ Are any students shy when presenting? Would they like a companion or the teacher to accompany them on stage or the presentation area?
◆ Does any presentation need support during the presentation?
◆ Do you have any students that have a language barrier? What assistance will they need during the presentation?

Presentation Day

The presentation day is the final day of the project and a big celebration day for all the eager learners. They are filled with excitement on this special day! Each student, partner pair, and group have the opportunity to stand in front of their peers and invited guests and share their expert knowledge of the topic and their final project creation. Students are usually eager and enthusiastic on this special day.

As presentations get underway, it's a perfect opportunity to teach audience behavior to students. Teach students to listen attentively to the speaker, make eye contact and consider the ideas the presenter is sharing; this seems to come a bit more naturally to children than adults. When each presentation concludes, invite a few members of the audience to ask the expert questions about their project. This presents the student with the opportunity to extend their ideas about the topic while they maintain their curiosity and wonder.

Also on display during presentation day are the incredible things the students have created, learned, and accomplished during the unit. The focus wall is one way to show and document all the learning from the unit. In addition to the focus wall, you want to have field guides, photographs of students immersed in the learning, books, completed drawings, etc. on display for the guests to learn more about the topic. This gives students the opportunity to share ideas from these areas with the guests after the presentations. Think of it as a gallery of the topic, where all student work, thoughts and ideas are on display.

Putting the Pieces Together

Each project-based unit is like a puzzle with different working pieces or a delicious pot of gumbo with hand-picked ingredients. Each unit contains different components, special discoveries and culminating projects that set it apart from the rest. This chapter is a glimpse of the planning process and some of the parts and pieces that can be considered as you plan your own project unit. As you begin the project planning process, consider where the suggested ideas from this chapter might fit into your project unit. Don't be afraid to try on different variations of the ideas presented and tailor them to fit your learners.

Chapter 4 Reflection

How have you considered approaching the planning process of your first unit?

When contemplating the three phases of PBL, what ideas are you thinking more about?

Inquiry Stations – Learning from the Childlike Mindset

FIGURE 4.9 A visit from turtle may spark ideas for a project unit!

What is interesting about this picture?

What might the child who found this turtle be wondering?

How might we apply our knowledge of creating a project unit and its three phases to this discovery? How would you begin planning a unit on turtles?

Reference

The Build Network staff. (2021, January 5). *You Cannot Solve What You Don't Understand.Inc.Com.* https://www.inc.com/thebuildnetwork/you-cannot-solve-what-you-dont-understand.html

5

Illuminating Learning

Lizzie: What is memorable about projects in your own classroom?

Jenny (PreK4) When we did our last unit on flowers, each child prepared for their culminating project. One of my students said, "I want to do a project about roots." I replied, "OK, great! What are the materials you'll need?" He said, "I need string," and then he started cutting the string and made groups of threes with the string. He made four groups of three pieces of string. Then he said, "I need something to put my roots on." I set out materials for him to choose something, and he picked popsicle sticks. Then he said, "Well, I need four popsicle sticks because I have four groups of three with my roots." Then I watched him glue the roots to the bottom of the popsicle sticks. Then he placed the popsicle sticks on the paper, fanned them out and connected them at the top like an actual plant; the roots were all fanned out at the bottom. It was so neat that he came up with that and incorporated math and multiplication in his project and conversation. It amazed me! Now, my family members are always asking me to tell them another story from a project-based lesson because the things that happen in our classroom are exceptional.

Nancie (PreK4) There are two projects that stand out.

DOI: 10.4324/9781003332541-5

One is the giant dragon the class created and then paraded around the school to celebrate the Lunar New Year. The students worked together to create the dragon with their ideas and skills. They learned about the reason for making the dragon and how to work together.

They exchanged ideas and were so excited during the entire process. They were proud to show off their creation to other classes around the school.

The second project is a student who created puppets of a flower and bee to reenact pollination from our unit on flowers. She asked for specific materials, colored, cut, and made the puppets independently. She then acted out how the bee pollinates the flower. She expressed what she learned to the entire class with confidence and expertise.

Remaining Inquisitive

In a unit of study on birds, when pondering why a duck beak or bill (we discovered a second name through our research) is different from a crane's beak, the eager four- and five-year-olds set off on a discovery to find the answer to this question. It was interesting because all students were gathered around the inquiry table amid a discovery day during Phase Two. They all offered different ideas and thoughts on the beaks during our whole-class investigations. Once we talked about their shapes, diet, and habitat, students began thinking about why each beak was unique to that bird. Then, as if a puff of fairy dust were sprinkled over their sweet little thoughts, they noticed and shared ideas that weren't considered in previous conversations. They built off each other's ideas to develop a whole-class response to the question "Why is a duck's beak different from a crane's beak?" They discovered that each bird's beak is unique because it has another job. A crane needs a beak that can plunge into the mud of a swamp or wetlands area to catch its food while a duck needs a beak that can strain out water from a scoop out of the bottom of a pond.

FIGURE 5.1 Students discover the differences in birds' beaks with a whole-class investigation.

The students' curiosity about the two beaks allowed for deep conversations during the whole-class discovery. As the teacher/facilitator, I was able to question them in a manner that truly made them think about the qualities of each bird and its beak. As we continuously provide opportunities for our students to stay curious about the world around them, we can support these efforts through questioning.

Questioning – A Key Role in Illuminating the Learning

In this chapter, we'll find out how questioning plays a huge part in project-based learning. A closer look into questions will reveal:

◆ What questions can we ask to help our learners stay curious?

◆ When should we ask exploration questions to help our learners think deeply about a topic?

I've heard it said a few times that questioning is one of the most challenging parts of project-based learning because there is no script, no prewritten questions and it requires the teacher to hold back from revealing the answers to their students.

Lizzie: What are the most challenging parts of project-based learning?

Lisette (PreK4): One of the most challenging things about project-based learning is pulling the learning out through questioning and allowing students to tell me more about the topic. I, the teacher, have all these great ideas to share and tell, but I have to remember that it's not my job to tell them the answers. So I work at questioning them with things like "What do you think?" and "What do you know?" And sometimes they stare at me like I'm speaking French or something. For example, one child was doing her final project on flowers, and we were talking about the materials she was planning to use in her model. She needed help deciding on her materials, and I wanted to tell her what to use for her flower, and I thought she could use a cupcake wrapper or something else round to represent the flower. Still, I stopped myself and realized that through questioning her, she'd be able to consider different options and decide how she'd best represent the flower.

Lizzie: I love that, Lisette. I think that's such a critical element that you bring up, and teachers need to hear that. I love hearing more about your active role in struggling through the idea of not giving the answers to your students but continuously striving to reach them through a deeper ponder of their ideas and wonders.

Pondering Our Conversation

I appreciate the idea that Lisette brings up about helping her student make decisions on representing her knowledge in the flower project. If Lisette had selected the materials for the student, she would have missed out on some valuable information from the learner.

1. Choosing the materials for the student would have hidden the student's ability to apply their learning to the final project. For example, the student might have considered the flower's shapes, colors, and functions while carefully choosing her material. By allowing the student to choose her materials and display her knowledge, Lisette assessed what was learned about the topic and saw the learning growth throughout the project. Instead of giving children certain materials and telling them where to place them, Lisette knew the value of questioning this student about what materials she thought would best represent the flower she wanted to create.

2. Through their conversation about materials and her knowledge of a flower, Lisette can assess the student's learning. If the student hasn't fully developed her understanding of the topic, Lisette will continue to support her through questioning and conversation.

What Questions Can We Ask to Help Our Learners Stay Curious?

Eleanor Roosevelt once said, "I think at a child's birth, if a mother could ask a fairy godmother to endow it with the most useful gift, that gift would be curiosity."

Staying curious about the world around us is a massive pillar in the entire project approach. It invites students to wonder, ponder and remain curious as they learn more about the world each day. As facilitators of learning, we play a role in continually asking our students questions about their learning. Our mission is to help our young learners consider ideas about the topic of study and guide them through questioning, to develop answers and responses to their wonders.

When thinking about how we might question students during a project unit, it's important to consider our approach to questioning. Just as we had to drop the role of sole information giver, it's important to consider dropping the idea that one size fits all learners. In thinking more about this idea, we discover that the use of only whole-class questioning doesn't always support each learner, their thought processes, and their ability to make meaning of the content. Through the practice of questioning our students individually and in smaller groups and partaking in conversations about the topic, we can focus on appreciating each child's creative abilities. As learners continue to make meaning with the project topic and information they are gaining, we can individualize and differentiate our instruction based on each child's needs. One way to do this is by emphasizing the questions we ask our learners each day.

I have a vivid memory of my first day in second grade. As I sat at my desk with my brand new crayon box and school supplies piled high, the teacher began asking us a round of questions. We would put our hand up if we knew the answer and leave it down if not. She asked, "What is the state flower of Louisiana?" My hand immediately shot up. I don't even know how I knew it, but I was sure I had the correct answer in my mind. To my surprise, she called on me, and I enthusiastically replied, "a magnolia." She smiled with delight and then moved on to the next question. I was so pleased with myself! The entire day, I kept thinking to myself, "Yes! I answered a question right." And when I got home from my first day of second grade, the first thing I shared with my mom was that I answered a question right. One question right! This memory has stuck with me all these years, not because I know my state flowers, but because as a continuous learner myself in education, I'm constantly considering what impactful teaching looks and sounds like.

Now, as I reflect back on that memory, I wonder a few things:

1. What have I done with that knowledge of knowing the state flower?
2. What was the result of knowing a basic recall question?
3. Has this experience helped to prepare me for questions about the world that I may not know?
4. What did I internalize about being right?

5. What happened to my fellow classmates in that moment? What if they didn't know the answer? How did it make them feel?
6. Did this experience push me to seek answers to other questions?

When considering how to support our learners to stay curious about the world around them, we can lean on robust questioning as a tool. In project-based learning, questioning can be used in a variety of ways.
We can question to:

◆ Find out what our learners already know
◆ Support individual learners or groups of learners in investigating their wonders
◆ Support our learners by modeling ways to continuously ask questions that lead to a clearer understanding of a topic
◆ Gain a glimpse of what they're learning throughout each phase of the project
◆ Help our students develop their ideas as they build their knowledge and work toward mastery

Questioning in a project-based unit is often open-ended, leaving the learner to ponder, investigate and discover possible outcomes. Our role as questioners of and cheerleaders for our learners is to inspire each child to embrace their creative ability and move forward as lifelong learners. Once a child is taught how to ponder the world around them and find the answers to their questions, he is set on a path filled with valuable learning opportunities for their entire life.

At four, the world is indeed a child's oyster. If you've been around a four-year-old long enough, you'd realize they wonder and ask about everything. This is such a celebration!

Let's spend a moment in a four-year-old and five-year-old's thoughts:

◆ Why is the sky blue?
◆ Why do dogs bark?

- ◆ Where does the water go after it leaves the sink?
- ◆ Why can't penguins fly?
- ◆ Why can't I eat ice cream for dinner?
- ◆ What makes a car go?
- ◆ How do owls see at night?
- ◆ And their list truly goes on and on, as they take in the beautiful world around them. We'll recognize this art of wonder in the 98% of four-year-olds scoring in the genius range when assessed by Drs. Land and Jarman (1992). How are we teaching students about finding answers to their questions, or, more importantly, what is their perception of how to go about finding solutions to these questions?

Do they think, "I can just ask my teacher, or mommy or daddy, and they'll tell me the answers," or are we teaching them how to wonder, investigate and put pieces of information together to answer questions. When we allow students room to wander and discover, we invite their creative abilities to shine and flourish.

When we begin at an early age to teach children how to investigate to find answers to their questions, we're essentially teaching them how to be independent thinkers and problem solvers. When a child wonders, "Why is the sky blue?" We can turn to the framework of project-based learning to help them find the answer to this question.

Through these deep conversations, observations, discoveries and research, children learn how to be profound thinkers.

In thinking more about that question, "Why is the sky blue?," It's important to consider how we might support the learner to discover more about this inquiry instead of focusing on them immediately knowing the answer. Through questioning, discovery, and research, our role is to give them the tools and show them how to be independent thinkers. You might follow up on their question: Why do you think the sky is blue? This question will help you see their misconceptions and support your efforts in clearing them up through discovery. Then, move into assisting them in finding out exactly why the sky is blue. Along your journey of discovery, continue to pose wonders to them instead of telling them the answers, even when it's a simple concept.

It's not about who's right but about how they set out to discover answers to their questions. This is independent problem-solving.

Each learner will require a different set of questions to move them along in their discovery. Project-based learning invites differentiation into your classroom on many different levels, one level is met through questioning. As you converse with your learners both as a whole group and individually, you'll find that your questions will vary based on the learner and their needs.

Supporting this type of wonder and curiosity could be supporting the next Albert Einstein – who gave us the Theory of Relativity – or Rosa Parks – who questioned equality on a simple bus ride. These are just two examples of the thousands of thinkers who challenged the world around them and persevered to find answers to those wonders. What if Rosa Parks had given up her seat without questioning this rule? How much longer would cause the unfairness of segregated bus rides have continued? Every child in your class has multiple gifts and talents, and we have the joyful job of helping to encourage the development of these gifts. Teaching our students to remain curious about the world around them and question thoughts and ideas helps nurture each remarkable talent.

Project-based learning enlists us, the teachers, to find the question that gets our students to think about their learning honestly. We have the fantastic opportunity to watch their thoughts and ideas blossom. Instead, when you may be tempted to think, "What should I ask them?," instead, turn that thought into, "Yes! I have the opportunity to consider a series of questions that will help this child cultivate a better understanding of this idea." There is no set recipe for the exact question you should ask; the only requisite is that you make time to ask it.

When Should We Ask Exploration Questions to Help Our Learners Think Deeply about a Topic?

"When should we ask exploration questions to help our learners think deeply about a topic?" is an important idea to consider continuously. In Phase One, we open the entire project unit with an overall question that all learners are working to discover. Whether we're working to figure out what makes frogs unique or why birds are different, this BIG question is posed to ignite a world of discovery. As the project moves forward, we support the cultivation of our learners, developing new ideas around the topic through the learning experiences we provide and the questions we ask them. During Phase Two, part of our role is to question the thoughts and ideas of our learners as they begin to make meaning around the topic. Then, even at the very end on presentation day, we can still pose questions to our project experts to glean some insight from their expertise. We are constantly asking our learners questions. So, the answer to our above-posed question, "When should we ask exploration questions?," is "Always."

When thinking about the journey it took each faithful builder in constructing the Great Pyramid of Giza, builders knew that each brick they placed on the first foundational row would be vital as they worked their way up to the top peak. Today's beautiful peak would have never stood tall if any brick had been omitted. Similarly, our work through the three phases of a project leads to a peak of understanding. Every thought, wonder, and discovery is a brick helping you and your students reach higher to the peak of understanding. Our questions help their understanding develop until they eventually reach their peaks.

I can remember my mother telling me stories about her childhood and particularly that in those days, the idea was that children should be seen and not heard. This meant that a lot of talking and chatter from a child was not welcomed. As we fast-forward many years ahead, project-based learning completely turns this idea of silent children around. We no longer want our students to "sit and get" information from us; instead, we invite them to find out the answers to their wonders. Our classrooms should no longer be quiet places: they should be happily noisy and centered around students talking about wonders and discoveries.

Asking Encouraging Questions

Since questioning leads to so many discoveries, our day must be filled with supportive questions to lead and guide our little learners. Our questions should often begin with why, how, and what you notice. Allowing our students time to ponder and consider an idea daily will strengthen their stamina during the discovery and inquiry parts of a project. As we partake in conversations with our students, whether in a whole group or on an individual basis, our conversations should be tailored to fit their needs for growth as learners. We can begin to scaffold their understanding of the topic through the questions we ask and through the questions our students start asking themselves.

Questioning Chatter – Setting the Scene for a Great Conversation

PBL Unit Topic: Sharks
Lens Over: A conversation during an inquiry station

The Scene: Students are in the middle of Phase Two, visiting inquiry stations about their unit topic, sharks. One student is in a station that highlights sharks' skin. This inquiry station is at a table in the classroom. On the table are books about a shark's skin, magnifying glasses, sandpaper, various samples of rough papers, photographs of a shark's skin up close, and various materials for making a patch of shark's skin. And there are also posed questions for the learner: What do you notice about a shark's skin? How might you make a miniature model of shark's skin using these materials? The teacher walks up and immediately begins conversing with one of the students at the table.

Teacher: What are you noticing about a shark's skin?
Student: That it looks smooth, but it's really not.
Teacher: What makes you think that?

Student: Well in the book, it shows me a close-up picture of a shark's skin and that's definitely not smooth like a rock. I think it looks like lots of sharp teeth right next to each other. I used my magnifying glass to take a closer look at the picture too.

Teacher: That's interesting! I wonder why a shark would have pointy skin. Where can we look to help us figure this out?

Student: I'm going to keep reading to search for more clues about a shark's skin. I think it's because it helps the shark swim in some way.

Teacher: That's an interesting idea. Let's read this page together to see what the shark expert author tells us about why its skin is kind of sharp. Teacher reads excerpt to student.

In the midst of reading: Student cheers and celebrates the information the teacher has read about sharks. "That's it! Their skin helps them move fast through the water and stay quiet. They need it to stay quiet to sneak up on fish."

Teacher: Great researching! What did the author call their bumpy skin?

Student: It's called den... den... dendrites.

Teacher: Dendrites, yes! What materials are you going to use to build a model of the shark's dendrites?

This conversation could have been accomplished in a completely different manner. The teacher could have told the students about a shark's skin and the name for the tiny scales all over its body, or they could have handed the student a worksheet that involved cutting and pasting labels of a shark's body; however, that would have taken away from supporting the student to be intrinsically motivated to wonder and discover. Through these deep conversations, we can help students navigate through the information they take in. Each talk looks and sounds different from the next. Each question is designed to fit that individual learner's need at the moment. All of our students are different in their learning abilities, and supporting their ideas through questioning is a fantastic way to meet each of them on their learning path and help them excel at their own pace.

Sparking Creative Abilities in Any Setting

One of the most beautiful things about project-based learning is that it can be used with anyone, at any time, and in any setting. If you're wondering where to begin or how to fit this into your current teaching environment, let's consider a few thoughts together.

Scenario One: I'm ready to jump in feet first with beginning project-based teaching and learning in my early childhood classroom.

Awesome! Remember, the project unfolds as you move through the three phases, don't be tempted to get discouraged or overwhelmed during any part of this fantastic learning journey. Think about the learning from Chapter 4 and the ideas presented in each of the three phases. Once you've selected your topic of study, you can begin the planning process using the topic web. Then you'll consider ideas and plans for each learning phase. You may try out one of the unit samplers at the very end of the book. The ideas in these completed units may help by walking you through the planning process, each of the three phases, and an overall glimpse of a unit. However you begin, whether writing your own or starting with one of the two units given in this book, start and jump in feet first. You'll learn so much from your students along the way.

Scenario Two: I'm thinking a little bit more about project-based learning and would like to incorporate aspects of it in my current thematic units or preschool curriculum before I plan a full unit. Is this a possibility?

Yes! Many parts of project-based learning can be incorporated into the current learning happening in your early childhood classroom. You may consider beginning with just a focus wall about your teaching content. This would allow students to interact with their learning and visually see the progress over the days of the unit. Let's pretend you were planning to teach a thematic unit on pumpkins in the fall.

In addition to your current plans, bring in project-based learning with strong visuals on a focus wall.

Remember the mission of the focus wall is to display learning and invite students to interact with the topic. You might consider a full-on focus wall that includes a title, real pumpkin photographs, a driving question and a thinking map made with the students and their discoveries all around it. As you get comfortable working with a focus wall, slowly begin to bring in other aspects of project-based learning. The following steps may be to think about an art project you've included in your thematic unit. What is the outcome of this art project? Will all students' artwork appear roughly the same? How might you harvest students' strengths in creativity while inviting a variety of lesson outcomes instead of the one polished product? There are many different paths for slowly bringing in pieces of project-based learning until you make your way to a fully immersed classroom working solely from a project-based framework.

Scenario Three: I would love to bring project-based learning into my daycare setting. Is this type of learning beneficial for my children?

Absolutely! An early learning daycare is a fantastic place to bring project-based learning to life. The students will be eager and ready to dive into various topics.

Daycare or childcare centers offer a large amount of learning time without disruptions. This makes for the perfect recipe for finding success in project-based learning. First, consider what instructional goals your daycare center encourages. Then see how you might align the current goals to the goals you'd like to set with project-based learning. I taught an entire project-based unit in a daycare setting, and it was such an amazing experience for both the students and me. They were eager to dive into our topic, discover through whole-group discovery days and learn more in inquiry stations. I heard repeatedly from parents that their children were coming home talking all about the topic and sharing new learning with them.

Lizzie: Is there anything you'd like teachers to know about project-based learning?

Lisette (PreK4): This is a teacher's opportunity to be creative. There are so many have-tos in education. You have to follow this script or this program, and there really aren't any have-tos in project-based learning other than how you have to let the kids guide the learning and you, the teacher, have to let go.

Jenny (PreK4): It's so cool to put learning in their hands and let them guide the learning. You can see the engagement they have throughout the unit. The conversations you overhear in the classrooms and even how they carry the learning out to the playground through conversations or extended learning is really cool.

Nancie (PreK4): I love that project-based learning allows students to learn by doing. Students explore, investigate, and work together to answer questions on a topic. It is rewarding to see them engaged and excited about learning.

Lillian (PreK4): What I love about project-based learning is that a particular topic is studied over time and that the children's prior knowledge and questions are part of the process. I definitely feel that this keeps the children interested in learning a particular topic. I also love that the children have choices about how they are going to learn the topic, because this keeps them motivated, and free to be creative.

You: What will be your response and reflection? What will you share with teachers about your journey in project-based learning? This is an exciting response to consider. I look forward to hearing more about the project experience in your early childhood classroom, daycare center, homeschool setting or Saturday afternoon project with your children or grandchildren.

No matter your educational setting and background, you can confidently take on planning, preparing and teaching either aspects of a project unit or an entire project with all three phases included. Planning a PBL unit is all about learning to navigate through a topic to maintain wonder and inquiry throughout the whole duration of the unit. Project-based learning is for everyone, and it harvests a natural creative ability in our youngest learners.

Questioning – Learning from the Childlike Mindset

What ideas are you considering as you ponder the role of questioning in a project unit?

How is this different from the methods of instruction often implemented?

References

Andersen, E. (2013, January 10). *10 quotes from the "First Lady of the World". Forbes.* https://www.forbes.com/sites/erikaandersen/2013/01/10/10-quotes-from-the-first-lady-of-the-world/?sh=6c4b8f25272b

History.com Editors. (2022, January 19). *Rosa Parks. HISTORY.* https://www.history.com/topics/black-history/rosa-parks

Land, G., & Jarman, B. (1992). *Breakpoint and Beyond: Mastering the Future Today.* HarperBusiness.

Wikipedia contributors. (2022, March 28). *Theory of Relativity. Wikipedia.* https://en.wikipedia.org/wiki/Theory_of_relativity

6

Achievable Documentation

Way back when, my grandmother, Baba, owned a famous bakery on a corner street in New Orleans. Her best-sellers were scrap cakes, wedding cakes, and eclairs. I heard many stories about the line that wrapped around the block just to buy a famous Weileman's Bakery pastry. My mom told us the same bakery stories over and over again, and every time we'd just soak in those precious memories. My siblings and I only knew about the bakery through stories. It was long closed before we were born. All we have are those stories from my mom. Stories about how my grandmother would pick every one of her employees each morning in her giant station wagon, feed them breakfast and lunch while they worked for her, and then load up once more for a drive home. My mom's job at the ripe old age of five was to stand on a wooden crate and greet every single customer that walked through the door. My grandmother made her say, "Good morning, welcome to Weileman's Bakery." Her goal was to make every customer feel welcomed and loved.

One of the most remarkable stories my mom told us was the story of the false teeth and the late-night robbery. A thief came into the bakery right at closing and demanded that the cashier give him money from the cash register. The cashier refused and was show in the mouth. Astonishingly, the cashier walked out of the bakery unharmed that night. The bullet lodged into his false teeth.

DOI: 10.4324/9781003332541-6

After the life-changing Category 5 Hurricane Betsy in 1965, my grandmother stood in the streets and gave away ice cream and cakes to the neighbors. She told of how grateful they were to have these sweets, since the power was out and food was scarce.

My grandfather Charlie was the original baker and taught my grandmother everything. When he got sick and could no longer run the bakery, my grandmother kept it going. Charlie was bedridden and kept his bed in the downstairs den right next to the bakery. Their home was attached to the bakery, so my grandmother was able to tend to him while continuing to keep the bakery running. As the head baker, Charlie kept all the recipes in his memory for years and years. When he was confined to his bed, my grandmother, and two other workers, would take turns visiting him during the day holding a pen and paper in hand. They'd say, "Charlie, we have to make brownies today, tell us what to do." My grandfather would begin listing off every ingredient and step-by-step guidance on baking the most delicious brownies. They would stand close by and write down every word he shared. This is how they retrieved all the famous recipes before his death. And when he passed on, my grandmother was still able to keep the bakery in business, using every one of my grandfather's original recipes.

What's the significance of these bakery day stories? Each story, memory, recipe, and picture shared is an important piece of documentation of a day in the life of Weileman's Bakery. Documentation provides us with valuable evidence and opportunity for reflection. A look back into these pieces of documentation would reveal the qualities of each person, their commitments, work ethic, care, treatment toward others, values and so many other ideals. The documentation of the daily happenings at Weileman's Bakery serve as information collected which clearly supports an image, a piece of history and important moments my family's past. Would we have all this information without the stories, pictures, and recipes? No, these beautiful memories would be lost forever. Documentation provides a view from many angles about a certain idea, piece of history, or, for us, a moment of learning.

These moments of learning happen every single day in our classrooms, and we have the joyful job of documenting the incredible flashes of learning that happen so frequently. Just as my mother and others have shared stories of the bakery days, we too can share stories, notes, and artifacts from the amazing learning taking place through the projects that happen in our classrooms. In this chapter, we'll build rationale around the importance and value of documentation through the three project phases.

What Does It Look Like?

Documentation takes a variety of forms in an early childhood classroom, especially one that focuses on project-based learning (PBL). It's important to note that there are a variety of ways in which we capture the learning progression during a PBL unit. Our students are constantly thinking, conversing, reading and creating; and it is important to document the students' learning journeys. Think of documentation as a museum exhibit where all the learning is on display and celebrated. Documenting student progress allows learners, teachers, and caregivers to gain a contextual understanding of student work that took place during the project, as well as the progressions the students made from start to finish.

Written and Note-Taking Documentation

Capturing the learning through note taking is especially important throughout each of the three phases of a project. We take notes as students struggle, succeed, discuss and discover. We, the observers, are continuously writing down what we see. This form of documentation is usually referred to as anecdotal note taking. During these observations, the teacher is collecting facts about what he/she has observed from individual students. Since this type of documentation is strictly factual, the notes are quick jots about a moment of learning. Observing and note taking is a daily occurrence through all three phases of the project.

I like to use a binder pre-loaded which includes a few observation sheets for every child in the class (See the online resources for printable documentation forms www.routledge.com/9781032355078). As a new project begins, you can begin a new note sheet for each child. This charts growth over time within each project topic and also allows the teacher to see growth over multiple projects and an extended period of time. At first, it may seem overwhelming to consider when these valuable observations can take place, considering the busy schedule and students' constant need of your support during the project. However, setting aside time each day to strictly observe and document, builds an appreciation for note taking as daily practice. Student observations become a key component of moving the project along, as new ideas about each child's learning progression are encountered and documented. These observations become a part of conversations with parents about their child's learning, co-workers about the developments observed, therapists to support their focused work on a specific child, administration when discussing student progress and the list of supports continues.

Verbal Documentation

Student talk begins in the first moments in the introduction of a new project and continues through the last phase of sharing expert knowledge. Students think aloud, ask questions, and discuss new learning throughout the entire unit.

Listening to student talk allows us to hear students' thinking process while they are independently and collaboratively inquiring, investigating, and creating. They build knowledge every day. As they talk, we listen for the important moments when students make a connection, support another student with evidence, or ask a thoughtful question. Recording highlights of student talk provides a window into their thinking and their progress in a unit.

Before engaging in PBL, I rarely documented things students said. I certainly didn't understand the value and importance in recording spoken thoughts onto paper. Once I leaned into PBL,

I couldn't imagine teaching without monitoring student learning through verbal documentation.

In considering what this might look like, we'll use a few examples for guidance.

One – Spoken thoughts, ideas or findings can be recorded as a blurb or caption to the bottom of their work, photograph or project. This caption is written by either the students or the teacher. This type of documentation brings pictures, drawings, or thoughts to life with explanations from the student.

For example: Look at this picture: What would you say about it? What is the child trying to convey? Is it clear? Yes, abstract art is wonderful, but that's not our purpose in viewing this picture. We want to understand and hear what the learner was thinking and how they were making meaning with their learning.

FIGURE 6.1 Painting of student work without an informational blurb to further explain.

Let's look at the picture a second time with an added caption. This time we'll see how documenting the learning heard in the classroom is a valuable way to make learning visible for all.

The hot air balloons are going up, because hot air makes things go up. This is a desert and the balloons are flying over the cactuses. The Ms are birds.

FIGURE 6.2 Painting of student work with an informational blurb to further explain the thinking behind the painting.

What are you thinking about? Did the caption give a snapshot of the learner's understanding? What have you now learned about the learner and their thought processes that you didn't know without that added caption?

Two – The documentation form mentioned earlier in this chapter is a perfect place to record what is overheard from conversations while students work. This gives a view into their thoughts about the topic. We gain strong insight by listening to our students. Simply jot down some of the conversations you hear happening each day. You won't need to jot down a response for every child, every day. Set a goal to observe a few students each week, until you've made notes on every child a few times throughout the project.

Three – Recording students' questions, thoughts, and findings on the focus wall allows all learners to revisit the ideas or make connections to the thoughts of their peers. Consider taping or stapling up slips of paper that contain bits and pieces of findings, conversations, and answers to questions overheard during the learning. Remember, the focus wall is an interactive support tool for the project. It doesn't need to be picture perfect, meaning you've neatly placed all the photographs and content on the wall in a strategic manner. Instead, students should be interacting with the focus wall by adding their learning daily. One way to add learning is through the addition of conversation snippet sheets that say what the child discovered, noticed, or answered with the name of child right next to the blurb. This type of documentation leads to extended learning, connections about content, and answers posed to questions.

Documentation through Photographs

A simple snapshot of learning in progress is one of the best ways to document the learning. Real-time photographs provide a clear glimpse into the work our students are immersed in throughout the project. Snapping pictures of conversations, inquiry stations, project creations, whole-class investigations, and field studies are an important way for students to see their learning in action. We want them to look at that picture and remember that moment of learning, remember what they were thinking and saying, and, most importantly, remember their connection to the learning. It's also a good idea to put these on display in your hallway or school office with other unit artifacts after the unit concludes. This allows others to connect with the learning happening in your classroom, while learning something new about the topic too.

FIGURE 6.3 Student working in an inquiry station.

After snapping this picture and adding it to the focus board, the teacher made this a conversational piece during whole-group conversation on the carpet. She invited the student to come up and share more about his creation in the inquiry station. He was so excited to share this snapshot of learning, smiling, he eagerly jumped up and made his way to the focus board. He went on to share more about his bird habitat creation, why certain birds lived in specific parts of the tree, and exactly how they built their nests. He also shared that the flower under the tree was filled with nectar for the hummingbird. It was a brief explanation packed with knowledge about the content. It gave the teacher an idea about his learning progression and, at the same time, shared valuable information with his classmates. This type of learning and connections would rarely be inspired by a worksheet or coloring sheet. This was a moment where a true link to learning happened and was captured by a quick snapshot.

Student Work – A Strong Piece of Documentation

Every drawing, excerpt in a field journal, painting, construction, and culminating project is a strong example of documentation. Not only does this type of work allow for a child to express him/herself creatively, but it also most undoubtedly documents their understanding. Through student work, we are able to learn so much about a child, their development in the topic, and their understanding of the content. We also see their creative side come to light through use of color, choice of artistic media, use of shapes, and a vision of how they bring their knowledge to life through their own creative work. Worksheets, packets, and directional art activities limit this type of creative ability and hide the true creative ability of our young learners.

I'll never forget the week my son came home with the same worksheet for five days in a row. It was a coin-counting worksheet, and he was asked to color the different coin faces a certain color. Dimes were colored blue, green for quarters, and so on. It came home on Monday, on Tuesday, and again on Wednesday. I thought, "surely this is it," but no, the same worksheet came home again on Thursday and Friday. Five sheets of copy paper that looked exactly the same and required exactly the same expectation five times. That's twenty-five copies on the copy machine a day, for the entire class, for five straight days in a row. Worksheets were a regular practice this particular year and I grew concerned about his ability to creatively express his understanding in this class. It appeared as though his thinking was being confined and limited by a printed sheet of paper, where he was expected to do the exact same thinking five days in a row. However, after day three, I began growing grateful for these worksheets. It was through this monotonous task that we realized that he was an amazing artist. After the students finished their work on that limiting piece of paper, they were allowed to draw on the back. I began looking forward to the heavy amount of worksheets that came home each week, because I learned that my child was truly gifted in drawing. He would draw the most intricate and amazing drawings full of detail and color. I didn't really know about his amazing artistic ability before this particular year. Imagine the opportunity for his creative ability to soar if he were immersed in a project-based approach where drawing, building and artistic ability were a daily occurrence.

FIGURE 6.4 Drawing to illustrate child's creativity on blank paper.

FIGURE 6.5 Drawing to illustrate child's creativity on blank paper.

When we provide our students with a variety of styles to express their knowledge and creative ability through their student work, we're opening doors that will lead them to wonderful learning opportunities. We learn so much about our students through their independent and group work. This form of documentation should happen daily throughout the project. We want to provide our students with opportunities to express their knowledge. This also serves as great formative assessment tool, as we gain insight to their mastery of the content. It's important to provide multiple opportunities for this type of creative expression throughout the project's three phases. In each provided opportunity, we learn more and more about our students.

Why document?

There are a million and one reasons why it's important and imperative to document learning, especially in an early childhood classroom. Let's focus on a few of these reasons and the support they provide in a project-based unit.

1. Documentation allows the teacher to see growth and progression through the unit and the entire year. When we provide students with opportunities to demonstrate their knowledge through a variety of means, we're collecting high volumes of data to support their academic and creative growth. In one classroom, students were studying ocean creatures. The teacher asked her students to draw an ocean creature on the first day of the project; this was so she could see their prior knowledge and assess their understanding. Later, in Phase Two, she asked them to draw the same ocean creature, but this time add in any new learning they may have picked up through Phases One and Two. This was interesting because the drawings completely shifted. Students spent a longer amount of time creating their drawings the second time. They added many details about the ocean creatures they learned about in the prior weeks during Phases One and

Two. The backgrounds in the drawings shifted as well, because they discovered more about the habitat of the specific ocean creature and included it in the background.

2. It's essential to the everyday work and planning of a project unit. When we carefully analyze our daily documentation, whether we're looking at student conversations or a drawing sample, we're able to tailor our lessons for each child based on the evidence their documentation provides. Our classrooms are filled with many different types of learners and through daily documentation we're able to support their unique needs.

3. We must know our learners, their abilities, their struggles and successes. It's through various forms of documentation provided on a daily basis, that we learn about each individual student in our classroom. We can never truly know each individual learner through limited forms of documentation, such as worksheets or step-by-step art activities. It's through open-ended learning opportunities that we truly gain an understanding of our students.

4. Collecting the many forms of documentation throughout the project unit are especially helpful when meeting with a data team, your grade-level team of teachers, administration, or a parent about a specific child or the growth of the entire class. It's through these work samples that all can distinguish the learning processes happening for each child and the class as a whole.

5. It provides pathways for other students. When we invite students to express their understanding in a variety of ways, we're also supporting learners' connections with their learning as they view and take in information from their classmates. Once students see what another classmate has created or how another child has expressed their knowledge, they begin making connections with their learning and understanding of the content. When we provide multiple opportunities for students to try on their learning and share these pieces of documentation, we're inviting all learners to make connections to each other's creations and extend their own thinking.

Putting All the Documentation Together

At the very end of a project, many teachers place creations, projects, drawings, focus wall, etc. on display somewhere in the school or their own classroom. This invites others to view all the documentation from the entire unit and celebrate the learning that happened over the last few weeks. Picture an entire wall and table covered in student drawings, culminating projects, charts containing student drawings and ideas, photographs of students discovering, blurbs sharing student conversations and findings somewhere in your school. It's an exciting picture to imagine! This is a celebration of true learning taking place, where each individual learning style is welcomed and cultivated.

After the project display has been shared with others in the school community, teachers often create project memory boxes and folders, and some even make scrapbooks. This practice documents each specific child's learning in that unit and is a forever memory of joyful learning for the child. Instead of sending home multiple worksheets that most often are thrown away, sending home a portfolio or memory box of the learning each child encountered throughout the unit, serves as documentation that can be revisited over and over again by the child and their family. Teachers often fill memory boxes/folders or scrapbooks with student work, pictures of the student engaged in learning, field study notebooks, blurbs of the child's conversations that once held an important spot on the focus wall, and anything else that contributes to documenting the wonderful learning that took place in that unit of study.

> I've learned that people will forget what you said, people will forget what you did, but people will never forget how you made them feel.
>
> – Maya Angelou

This is our goal! This is our final destination in project-based learning.

How have made our learners feel about learning more about the world around them?

What was it about a specific project that brings back memories of joy?

We want to make our learners feel joyful about constantly learning about the beautiful world around them. Daily immersion in project-based learning creates these opportunities for our youngest learners. They won't remember the joy of learning from a worksheet or the invitation to be creative from a coloring sheet, but they will remember the experiences that project-based learning brought to their early childhood classroom every single day! These memories and experiences will provide students will the tools to be successful life-long learners.

Documenting the Learning – Learning from the Childlike Mindset

What forms of documentation are you familiar with in your own learning setting?

What forms of documentation are you thinking a little more about incorporating into your learning setting?

What forms of documentation invite a child to remember the amazing joys of learning?

Reference

Kogan, Y., Chard, S., & Castillo, C. A. (2017). *Picturing the Project Approach: Creative Explorations in Early Learning*. Gryphon House.

7

Project-Based Learning Unit Samplers

Lizzie: What might you say to a teacher that may be considering planning and teaching their very first problem-based learning (PBL) unit?

Nancie: I would say that it might seem a little intimidating at first, but well worth the time and effort it takes to implement a PBL unit. Observing the light bulbs that go off in your students' heads and the learning and knowledge that they get from this way of teaching is amazing and wonderful! Observing the students interacting and talking with each other about the unit topic is fantastic.

Lisette: It's organic, there's not a formula for PBL! This is the teacher's opportunity to be creative too! You have to let go and let the kids guide!

Jenny: I love that Lisette, yes, you must let go. It's really cool to hear the students' engagement in the project topics. They love it! Their conversations about learning even carry out to the playground and carpool.

Lillian: The children will love it and be very enthusiastic about learning! I love that in project-based learning a particular topic is studied over time and that the children's prior knowledge and questions are part of the process. I definitely feel this keeps the children interested in learning a particular topic. I also love that the children have choices about how

DOI: 10.4324/9781003332541-7

they are going to learn the topic, because this keeps them motivated, and free to be creative.

In the previous six chapters of this book, we've carefully considered ideas for bringing project-based learning into your learning space. Project-based learning is truly a celebration of wonder and discovery each day for our little learners. As you continue to consider and ponder the learning in the previous chapters, use this chapter as a guide to get started. In this chapter, you'll find two PBL full unit samples. Each unit will offer a day-by-day plan for the three phases of project-based learning, as well as sample pictures and ideas to help you get started. You might consider teaching one or both units, so you can get a feel for what and entire unit looks, before jumping in to plan your own unit. You'll notice that there will be some similarities and differences in both units. This is to show you that no two units are exactly alike or include all of the same ideas. You may consider using both units in their entirely, before you begin planning your own project unit, or incorporate some of the ideas from these units into your current curriculum.

Unit One: Birds
Project Based Learning Unit Sampler 1
Project Topic – Birds
Timeline: 15 days

Overview: In the project-based unit on birds, students will investigate and discover the many types of birds and their special traits. Throughout the three phases of this project, students will discover more about many different birds, their habitats, their diet, their special features, and their role on the earth. This unit is fun and filled with many opportunities for creative expression as well as deep thinking. Also included in this unit are real photographs from an early childhood classroom where this unit was taught.

Driving Question: What makes birds special?

Picture books to support all three phases throughout unit:

◆ *The Beak Book* by Robin Page (2021)
◆ *Beaks!* by Sneed Collard (2002)
◆ *Birds Make Nests* by Michael Garland (2019)

- *Nesting* by Henry Cole (2020)
- *Peep Inside a Bird's Nest* by Anna Milbourne (2022)
- *Mama Build a Little Nest* by Jennifer Ward (2014)
- *Birds in my Backyard* by Lisa Donovan (2021)
- *All the Birds in the World* by David Opie (2020)
- *Big Book of Birds* by Yuval Zommer (2019)
- *Penguins* by Anne Schreiber (2009)
- *Bird Nests and Eggs* by Mel Boring (1998)
- *Feathers Not Just for Flying* by Melissa Stewart (2022)
- *Hooray for Birds* by Lucy Cousins (2018)
- *Bring on the Birds* by Susan Stockdale (2013)
- *A Nest Full of Eggs* by Priscilla Belz Jenkins (2015)
- *National Geographic Little Kids First Big Book of Birds* by Catherine Hughes (2016)

Phase One – An Immersion into Learning More about Birds

The planned duration for Phase One (the immersion phase) is four days. In these four days, students will be introduced to many types of birds through real photographs, books, and planned conversations. During Phase One, the teacher will begin observing and documenting the learning of each child as they progress through the unit.

TABLE 7.1
Layout of Phase One in bird unit.

Phase One	Day 1	5 Discovery Steps
	Day 2	5 Discovery Steps
	Day 3	4 Discovery Steps
	Day 4	4 Discovery Steps

The documentation log from Chapter 6 is a great place to begin.
Phase One Materials:

- Collection of picture books about birds on display in the room
- Real photographs of a variety of bird types, printed and laminated in various sizes
- Chart paper
- Bird artifacts: bird houses, model of fake bird's nest, stuffed animals or figurines of birds, bird seed, etc.

- Selected spot for focus wall
- Topic (Birds) labeled at the top of focus wall
- Magnifying glasses

Phase One – Day One

Prepping for the day: Before students enter the room on day one, you'll want to have the beginnings of your focus wall set up and in place. This includes a title, "Birds," photographs hanging around the wall, and the project message. If your wall is low, the project message can hang right on the board, if your board placement is up higher, the project message will need to be either on an easel or an area where students have the ability to write as well.

Discovery Step #1: The first project message of the unit will be the opening to today's learning. You'll want to have parts of the message prewritten on chart paper, before the students enter the room that day and the children will help with fill in the remainder of the wording during the conversation. This is a perfect time to bring your own creativity to light. Feel free to add in visuals to your project message as often as possible. Make it colorful and inviting to student learning. As you prepare to read and converse together about the project message, you'll want to gather students together in a central meeting area, where they can turn and talk with a

FIGURE 7.1 Sample project message written on chart paper.

partner. Turn and talks will be a daily instructional strategy we'll incorporate into many of our learning opportunities.

> **Project Message Idea:**
> Good Morning Discoverers,
> Today we will start learning about birds and what makes them special!
> Think about a bird and draw it.

Gather students together and read the project message aloud. You'll notice many of them try to read right along with you! You may consider using a pointer as you track the words and read aloud. On the bottom portion of the message, where it invites learners to draw or tell about a bird, you may consider three ways to accomplish this task.

1. Give each child a sticky note and ask them to draw their bird on the sticky note. Then as they come up to add their drawing, they can share more about what they drew.
2. Invite a few students up at a time to draw their birds directly on the chart paper.
3. Let students help you construct the ideas to write.

Discovery Step #2: After all students have added their bird drawing to the project message, ask students to turn to their talking partner on the carpet or meeting space. Ask them to share a time that when they have seen a bird and what they noticed about it.

Discovery Step #3: Read a selected non-fiction book about birds. You'll want to choose something that gives an overall glimpse of birds. It might include information that tells more about all birds, instead of focusing on one specific bird. As you read, stop and invite students to share ideas and converse together.

Discovery Step #4: A gallery walk of bird pictures. Hang up various bird photographs around the room and invite students to walk with their partner around the room visiting each bird photograph and stopping to chat about what they notice. You might consider playing classical or low music as they walk and share. While students are conversing during the gallery walk, you can listen in on conversations and begin documenting their ideas and wonders.

Discovery Step #5: Bringing day one to a close – After the gallery walk has been finished, gather students once more in the central meeting space. Invite them to share ideas from the photographs they visited. What did they notice? What was interesting about the photograph? What are they still wondering? You might even bring some of the photographs from around the room to the center of the conversation circle, so students can reference them as they share ideas.

> As the first lesson of the birds project comes to a close, you'll want to move the bird pictures to the focus wall and hang the first of many project messages near the focus wall. Also consider writing down some of the ideas students share about the bird pictures from their gallery walk on sentence strips or blank sheets of paper. Then, hang their observations next to the bird pictures on the focus wall.

Phase One –Day Two

Prepping for the day: In today's project-based learning lesson, students will continue to develop their knowledge of birds and begin to clear up any misconceptions. Today we'll continue adding to the focus wall, share bird knowledge on a circle map, and participate in conversations about birds with friends. Before the lesson, you'll want to have a circle map drawn on chart paper with birds written in the middle. You'll also want to have a pretty amazing bird story to share with students.

Discovery Step 1: Gather students together in the central meeting space in your classroom/learning space. Read a selected non-fiction book on birds. This book can focus on a specific type of bird or all birds in general. As you read aloud to your students, stop throughout the text to model your thinking about birds.

For example: Teacher pauses from book, looks up at his/her students, and models thinking aloud,

> I see that this bird has a curved beak and the text said it eats nuts and fruit, but the bird on the other page had a long straw like beak for sipping nectar. I'm realizing that all birds don't have the same beak.

I wonder what you're realizing as we read to find out more.

Discovery Step 2: Invite students to share ideas about what they know or are learning about birds. You'll record their ideas on the circle map. You may consider inviting a few students up to the circle map to draw what they've shared on the circle map. This map can be continuously added to as students discover more about birds though the unit.

FIGURE 7.2 Sample focus wall featuring photographs, charts, and student work samples.

Discovery Step 3: Dramatic Play with Birds – After growing their content knowledge and chatting more about the ideas presented in the book, invited students to consider movements of birds. As students consider and discuss bird movements, encourage them to move around the room acting like a bird.

Bird Movements to Consider: flying, standing on one leg (flamingo), pecking a hole in a tree (woodpecker), perching on a branch, sipping nectar from a flower (hummingbird), flying in a V shape.

Discovery Step 4: In the share part of today's lesson, it's important to get students talking about their learning. Bring them back to the central meeting space and tell a special story about a time you saw a bird and what it was doing.

Sample Story: One summer afternoon, I was taking a walk to the park in our neighborhood. As I entered the park, I saw a green bench and sat down. I was looking around at all the beautiful trees and saw a bird flying in and out of the tree. After it flew back into the tree the fourth time, I noticed it had something in its mouth. I kept watching it to find out what it was carrying. I realized it was sticks from the ground of the park. This little bird was making a nest in the tree in the park. He was working so hard carrying each stick in his beak back to the nest in the tree.

Invite students to think about a time they saw a bird, be sure to give a few minutes of wait time for their thinking. Then ask students to turn to a partner and share their story. Our goal is to hear a variety of stories about where birds live and their interactions in their habitats.

Discovery Step 5: In the final piece of today's learning, students will spend time reading and looking through a variety of books on birds. They can be fiction and non-fiction books on a wide variety of bird types or general bird information. Consider inviting student buddy pairs to choose a bird book from the book display area and read together to find out more about birds.

Phase One – Day Three

Prepping for the day: In the third day of the unit, students will continue to develop their knowledge of birds through a closer glimpse into some of their habits and behaviors. Today's learning will incorporate a math graph, as well as a drawing to collect their prior knowledge and assess their understanding of bird habitats. Before the lesson, you'll want to have the project message written, bird chart template created on large chart paper, a non-fiction bird book selected to read, and plain paper for drawing.

Discovery Step 1: Gather students together and begin reading the project message aloud to students. Remember to use a pointer as you track the words aloud with your students. Invite them to read along with you, they love this!

Project Message Idea:
Good Morning Feathered Friends,
Yesterday, we used our arms as wings to pretend to fly like birds. What did you notice about flying?
    Can all birds fly?

| Yes | No |

After students have considered their answer to this question, invite them up to write their name under the "Yes" or "No" columns. After all students have answered "shared the pen" by placing their name on the chart, begin conversation about the data on the chart with questions to the learners.

How many friends think all birds can fly?

How many friends think some birds cannot fly?

If you answered "No," why did you choose this? What birds do you know that cannot fly?

Add their data discoveries to the chart as they converse. Hang the chart near the focus wall after the discussion.

Discovery Step Two: Read a non-fiction book about birds aloud to the students. As you read aloud, stop throughout the book and notice and wonder ideas. You might consider modeling what it looks like to notice and wonder while reading. If you happen to come across any new bird vocabulary words, now is the perfect time to begin adding student-friendly definitions to the focus wall. Remember, the teacher writes the word if the child cannot, and the students draw out their definition. After one student has drawn the kid-friendly definition, the vocabulary card is added to the focus wall. As words come up through the unit, definitions are continually being added to the focus wall.

Discovery Step Three: Send students back to their workspace or table. Pass out plain paper and ask them to think about a specific bird and its habitat. Invite them to draw the bird in its habitat on the plain paper, using crayons, markers or colored pencils. As students draw, you'll want to walk around conversing with them about their drawing and documenting their understanding in your observation binder. This is an important step, because it's a window into their understanding of birds. We learn about students and their knowledge of birds in their habitats.

Discovery Step Four: After all drawings are complete, place students in groups of three or four. Encourage them to share more about their drawing and their details of the bird they included its habitat. As groups listen to students sharing, invite them to ask questions to the speaker about their drawings, offer suggestions to add to the picture, or share ideas about changing wrong information. For our little learners this sharing step may seem overwhelming, but the more we incorporate this into our teaching and learning environment, the more comfortable our students are about sharing, asking questions, and offering guidance. This is an important step in releasing responsibility to our young learners as we encourage them in speaking and listening. In a final question to the entire class, revisit the unit's focus question, "What makes birds special?," and listen in on their remarks. You might consider writing some of these ideas down and placing them near the question on the focus board. You'll see that each day, you add a little more information and student interaction the to focus board.

Phase One – Day Four

Prepping for the day: Day four is the last day in Phase One; tomorrow, the unit will move into Phase Two. Today, we'll give students the opportunity wonder and ask questions, observe bird artifacts and other hands on bird figurines. In preparation for today's learning, create a bird wonders chart, select a non-fiction book about birds, gather bird artifacts.

Discovery Step One: Gather students together in a circle in the central meeting space. Focus their attention to the wonders chart. Say,

> We've been discovering so much about birds over the last three days. When we learn about things, it's important to ask questions and then research to find out the answers to our questions. "What do you wonder about birds?" "What would you like to find out more about?"

Then have them turn and share a wonder with their buddy. You'll want to listen in on their wonders and shared conversations. After students share their wonders, record their questions on the wonder chart. Their wonders will be referred to often throughout the remainder of the unit. As the whole class, groups of students or individuals find answers in their research during Phase Two, you'll write or draw the answers and add them to the focus board.

FIGURE 7.3 Teacher listening in on student conversations during a buddy share.

Discovery Step Two: Read a non-fiction book about birds aloud to the students. Continue to notice and wonder as you read. Also, continuously look for opportunities to add to the vocabulary wall.

Discovery Step Three: In the final parts of Phase One, we'll present students with the opportunity to observe bird artifacts. You might consider putting the artifacts in the center of the circle or spread them out across tables for students to view and discuss. Invite students to observe and explore artifacts with classmates. They should be noticing and sharing with their friends around the table. Student conversations can be supported with conversational stems.

Conversational Stems: I see _____.
I wonder _____.
I think _____.

Discovery Step Four: Allow students to share their observations about the bird artifacts. Place the bird artifacts near the focus wall on a small table or at the top of a bookshelf for the duration of the unit. Students will revisit these artifacts in the next few days.

Phase Two – Discovery, Inquiry and Innovation

The planned duration for Phase Two (the inquiry phase) is eight days, beginning with day 5 of the unit and lasting until day 12. These eight days will be packed with inquiry, discovery, investigations, stations, and project creations. Students will discover more about birds through field site visits, virtual field trips, class investigations, inquiry station visits, and ending with their project creations. During Phase Two, the teacher will provide discovery opportunities, observe learners and document the learning and support learners in creating a model to share their expert knowledge on birds.

TABLE 7.2
Layout planning for Phase Two of bird unit

Phase Two	Day 5	5 Discovery Steps + Inquiry Stations
	Day 6	6 Discovery Steps + Inquiry Stations
	Day 7	5 Discovery Steps + Inquiry Stations
	Day 8	4 Discovery Steps + Inquiry Stations
	Day 9	5 Discovery Steps + Inquiry Stations
	Day 10	4 Discovery Steps + Inquiry Stations
	Day 11	4 Discovery Steps
	Day 12	3 Discovery Steps

Phase Two Suggested Materials:

♦ Collection of non-fiction books on birds displayed in the room
♦ Real photographs of a variety of bird types, printed and laminated in various sizes
♦ Chart paper
♦ Bird artifacts: bird houses, model of fake bird's nest, stuffed animals or figurines of birds, bird seed, etc.
♦ Clipboards
♦ Binoculars
♦ Brown paper, large cardboard box, sticks
♦ Possible beak examples: straws, serving tongs, scoop, etc.
♦ Field guide – recording sheets for three days of bird observations
♦ Large brown shopping bags (one per child)
♦ Linking cubes for measuring
♦ Art supplies – crayons, markers, colored pencils, paint, etc.

Note – additional materials are needed for inquiry stations and the culminating project. Those materials are listed in the correlating pages following.

Inquiry Stations

At the end of days 5–10, students begin rotating through the six stations at the end of the daily lesson. Learners will visit one station a day, cycling through all six across the next six days. In order to prepare and prep the inquiry stations, you'll need to gather materials for each station, set them up in various locations around the room, and leave them up for the duration of the next six days. Each station will contain its own materials, driving question or wonder and activity. Consider looking at your class list and making a rotation schedule with groups of four or five students moving to each station daily. You'll want to keep track of who visited which stations throughout the unit.

Station One: Bird Beaks

FIGURE 7.4 Inquiry station – Discovering more about bird beaks!

Bird Beak Station Materials:

- ♦ Linking blocks
- ♦ Straws, scoops, spoons
- ♦ Figurines of birds
- ♦ Markers, crayons, colored pencils
- ♦ Station guide
- ♦ Bird beak observation and recording page
- ♦ Photographs of different bird beaks
- ♦ Picture books on bird beaks:
    The Beak Book by Robin Page (2021)
    Beaks! by Sneed Collard (2002)

Inquiry Station Set Up: Choose a location in the classroom to set up this station. Set out bird photographs, building materials, recording sheet, magnifying glasses, figurines, markers, etc. Also create a station guide that explains to students what they will be discovering in that station.

Suggestions for Station Guide:

1. What do you notice about bird beaks?
2. Can you build different bird beaks?
3. Can you draw different bird beaks?

Inquiry Station Experience: We want our little learners to truly have an up-close look into why birds' beaks are different. We want them to notice their shapes, sizes, colors and, ultimately, their purposes. When students visit the bird beak station, they should begin with looking carefully at the photographs of bird beaks and reading about them by looking at the different beaks in books. Then, learners will use the given materials to build and create different beaks. Finally, they will draw the different beaks on their recording page. These pages can be hung around the room or near focus wall.

Station Two: Nest Building

FIGURE 7.5 Inquiry station – Observing and building a bird's nest.

Nest Building Station Materials:

- Yarn in various colors
- Twigs and sticks
- Brown construction paper
- Modeling dough
- Fine motor tweezers
- Station guide
- Small paper plates
- Photographs of bird nests
- Popsicle sticks
- Picture books on nests:
    Birds Make Nests by Michael Garland (2019)
    Nesting by Henry Cole (2020)
    Peep Inside a Bird's Nest by Anna Milbourne (2022)
    Mama Build a Little Nest by Jennifer Ward (2014)

Inquiry Station Set Up: Choose a location in the classroom to set up this station. Set out bird nest photographs, yarn, sticks, paper plates, and modeling dough. Also create a station guide that explains to students what they will be discovering in that station.
Suggestions for Station Guide:

1. What do you notice about a bird's nest?
2. What materials will you use to build a nest?

Inquiry Station Experience: In this station we're providing the opportunity for our learners to internalize what it's like for a bird to build a nest with its beak and feet. We want them to notice the shape and structure of different nests. When students visit the bird nest station, they should begin with looking carefully at the photographs of bird nests and reading about them. Learners will use the given materials to build a bird's nest just like a bird. They will use the fine motor tweezers to pick up their materials and create the nest on the paper plate. They can use the modeling clay to create eggs in the nest.

FIGURE 7.6 Inquiry station product – A bird's nest.

Station Three: Bird Habitats

FIGURE 7.7 Inquiry station – Bird habitats.

Nest Building Station Materials:

- ◆ Bird figurines
- ◆ Modeling clay
- ◆ Small pieces of cut yarn
- ◆ Plastic toy tree or connecting blocks
- ◆ Station guide
- ◆ Photographs of different bird habitats
- ◆ Sheets of blue felt
- ◆ Picture books on bird habitats:
  Birds in my Backyard by Lisa Donovan (2021)
  All the Birds in the World By David Opie (2020)

Inquiry Station Set Up: Choose a location in the classroom to set up this station. Set out materials to invite play with the bird figurines. Create a station guide that explains to students what they will be discovering in that station. Suggestions for Station Guide:

1. How does a bird's habitat help them live?
2. What do birds do all day?
3. Can you pretend with the birds?

Inquiry Station Experience: In this station we're providing the opportunity for our learners to learn through role play about a bird's habitat. We want them think about a day in the life of a bird and bring the figurines to life by building their nests in trees, pretending to be a penguin swimming through the ocean, making a flower for a hummingbird to sip nectar, etc. Learners will use the given materials to discover more through play.

Station Four: Watercolor Birds

FIGURE 7.8 Inquiry station – Watercolor birds.

Nest Building Station Materials:

- ◆ Watercolor paints
- ◆ Paint brushes
- ◆ Watercolor paper
- ◆ Water dishes
- ◆ Station guide
- ◆ Photographs of a variety of bird types
- ◆ Picture books about birds
    Big Book of Birds by Yuval Zommer (2019)
    Penguins by Anne Schreiber (2009)

Inquiry Station Set Up: Choose a location in the classroom to set up this station. Set out bird photographs, paint, paintbrushes, and dishes of water. Also create a station guide that explains to students what they will be discovering in that station.

Suggestions for Station Guide:

1. What do you notice about the colors of birds' feathers?
2. Which bird will you paint on your paper?

Inquiry Station Experience: This station is all about the celebration of the beauty of birds. We want them to notice the shapes and coloring of birds' feathers. As students visit the bird painting station, they will observe photographs of different birds and look at pictures of them in books. Learners will use the vibrant colors to bring birds to life on their blank papers.

Station Five: Birds in Shapes
Bird Shape Station Materials:

- Shape tiles
- Blocks
- Colored paper cut into shapes
- Station guide
- Tangram pieces
- Photographs of a variety of bird types
- Board and simple books on birds
  Birds by Kevin Henkes (2017)
  Curious About Birds by Cathryn Sill (2020)

Inquiry Station Set Up: Choose a location in the classroom to set up this station. Set out bird photographs, blocks, shape tiles, colored paper, etc. Also create a station guide that explains to students what they will be discovering in that station.
Suggestions for Station Guide:

3. What shapes do you see in birds?
4. What shapes can you use to create birds?

Inquiry Station Experience: This station is all about using shapes to create birds. This requires students to know the attributes of each shape and how they work together to create new shapes. After looking at pictures of birds, we invite learners to discover more about the body shapes of birds by creating them with blocks, tangram pieces, etc.

Station Six: Close Up on Bird Eggs

Bird Shape Station Materials:

- ◆ Photographs of different bird eggs
- ◆ Models drawn with paper of bird egg sizes
- ◆ Birds and their eggs match game
- ◆ Station guide
- ◆ Modeling clay
- ◆ Bird egg recording sheet
- ◆ Picture Books on Bird Eggs:
    Bird Nests and Eggs by Mel Boring (1998)

Inquiry Station Set Up: Choose a location in the classroom to set up this station. Set out bird egg photographs, models, matching game, etc. Create a station guide that explains to students what they will be discovering in that station. Suggestions for Station Guide:

1. What do you notice about bird eggs?
2. Can you match the birds to their eggs?
3. Can you make a bird egg with modeling dough?
4. Draw your observations of different bird eggs.

Inquiry Station Experience: This station introduces bird observers to the different shapes, sizes, and colors of bird eggs. It allows students to engage in deep observations about similarities and differences. After looking at pictures of bird eggs, students will observe the different shapes, sizes, and colors of eggs. Then, if you have a bird egg matching game (can be purchased on the internet) students can engage in that activity first. If not, then learners can go directly to making their own bird eggs with modeling clay, using the pictures as a guide. Last, learners will draw their observations.

Phase Two – Day Five

Prepping for the day: This is the first day in Phase Two and the fifth day of the unit. The next few days will look a whole lot different from the previous four days of the unit. In preparation for the beginning of Phase Two, all six inquiry stations should be completely set up with all materials in place and ready for discovery, before day five begins. In preparation for day five, the project message should be written ahead of time with areas for student interaction. Also, clipboards, observation papers, binoculars, and pencils should be easily accessible and ready. As we enter a new phase and continue our learning about birds, students will observe birds outside each day for the next three days. Consider playground bird observations or another area around your learning environment for students to observe and record.

Discovery Step #1: Invite students to the central meeting space and read the project message together. Pause and invite students to "share the pen" and add to the message with their drawings and letters. Share with students that they will be going outside to watch birds today and record their observations on a recording sheet. Remind students that we are all working together to find out what makes birds special.

Project Message Idea:
Good Morning Bird Watchers,
Yesterday we discovered more about birds.
Birds have _____.
Most birds can _____.
Today we are going outside to watch birds. What do you think we'll observe?

Discovery Step #2: With pencils, clipboards, recording sheets, and binoculars in hand, take students outside to observe birds in their environment. Plan to spend about 15 to 20 minutes outside observing birds in their environment, talking with students about what they see, and encouraging them to record their observations by drawing what they see in their field guide.

FIGURE 7.9 Child using binoculars to observe birds in their natural habitat.

FIGURE 7.10 Students working recording observations in their field guides.

Discovery Step #3: After spending enough time outside observing and discussing birds, bring learners inside and return to central meeting location. Invite learners to turn and talk with carpet partner about their observations. After students have shared, ask some students to share their observations with the entire class.

FIGURE 7.11 Students are working with a partner to share their observations.

Discovery Step #4: It's time to bring the bird observations to life! Invite students to act out what they observed birds doing outside. Talk about the birds' movements and patterns observed as they moved.

Examples: Did the bird fly back and forth from a location? Did the bird sit for a while on an electrical wire, fence board or another area? Did the bird fly in a specific pattern in the sky. Did a group of birds fly in a pattern?

Discovery Step #5: A focus on bird wings. Lay out different bird photographs and ask students what they notice about the different wings of birds. Invite students to share their observations. Read a non-fiction book focusing on bird wings or watch an expert short video explaining different birds' wings.

Display the bird wing (can have chart) and work together with students supporting them in facilitating the conversation about what bird wings can do and what they have. Fill in the chart as students share ideas. Explain to learners that they are going to create their own set of giant bird wings from what they've learned. Each student should receive a precut brown paper bag. Instruct them to use their knowledge and pictures around the room to draw the back of the bird with the wingspan spread open. You may want to mode this step, before you release them to draw on their own. Students can then color their wingspan with markers or crayons. As students complete their wings and are busy coloring the feather coloration, you'll want to assist them in cutting out their giant wingspan. The final step will be to attach strips of cardstock or strips of the left-over bag to the inside of the wingspan as handles. Once all wingspans have been cut out, invite students to lay their wings on the floor and use linking cubes to measure their wingspan. If there is available time, consider creating a chart that shares each child's wingspan, linking cube measurements.

Stations – Learners will move to their first round of stations. They will visit one station each afternoon over the next six days and rotate through all six by the end. Students should rotate with the same friends for the duration of the six days. You'll want to be sure to communicate each group's station for the day and where they'll rotate the next day to avoid confusion. Students should be spending between 10 and 20 minutes in stations each day. Remember, during inquiry stations, the teacher's role is to support the work in each station, observe the learning and document observations. Do you have an assistant that can serve in this same role as well?

Phase Two – Day Six

Prepping for the day: In the second day of Phase Two, students will again take their field guides outside to observe birds in their natural habitat. You'll also want to research a child-friendly video of a bird building a nest. Finally, learners will participate in a nest-building group project. You'll need materials organized and ready. Ideas for a large nest in the classroom: a large cardboard box as a base, large sticks or twigs, long strips of brown construction paper, long strips of fabric precut.

Discovery Step #1: Invite students to the central meeting space and read the project message together. Pause and invite students to "share the pen" and add to the message with their drawings and letters.

> **Project Message Idea:**
> Bird Observers,
> Yesterday we observed birds in their natural habitats.
> What are some bird habitats?

Discovery Step #2: Is there another location on your campus or around your learning environment where you can take students to observe birds? If possible, plan to take students to another location for bird observations today; if not, the same observation space will do. Before taking students out for their bird observation field study, you may consider talking with them about carefully observing bird patterns and movement today as they record in their field guide.

Observers will need clipboards, field guides (working on a new recording sheet), binoculars, and pencils, as they prepare for another great day of bird observations. Spend another 15 to 20 minutes outside observing, recording, and discussing birds in their habitats.

Discovery Step #3: After spending time outside observing birds in their natural habits bring students to the central meeting space and chat about what they observed today. Ask students if they observed anything different about birds than in yesterday's observations. Check the wonders chart on the focus board to see if there are any questions that can be answered from the observations.

Discovery Step #4: Share with learners that today they'll be taking an up-close look at how some birds build their nests. You might ask them to share what they know about nest building before they watch the video of a bird building its nest. Play the expert video for students and chat about what they are discovering as they learn more about how birds build a nest.

Discovery Step #5: Dramatic Play: Share with students that they will pretend to be birds and wear their bird wing creations from yesterday to build a large nest. Show them the possible building materials and talk about how their knowledge of nests and the expert video will them pretend to be birds and build their nests. Remind students that they are working together as a team. If you're class size is too large to build one giant nest, you may consider dividing students up into two, three, or four groups with multiple large birds' nests. Remember to take photographs of students creating nests to document the learning and share their experiences with others, document what students are saying as they build, and question them throughout the process.

Discovery Step #6: After the large nest creations have concluded, bring students together to share more about their experience as a bird, the teamwork they used to build together, and what they noticed about the difficulty in creating and building.

Stations – Learners will move to their second round of stations. Groups should be rotating through a different inquiry station each day. Students should rotate with the same friends for the duration of the six days. You'll want to be sure to communicate each group's station for the day and where they'll rotate the next day. Students should be spending between 10 and 20 minutes in stations each day. Remember, during inquiry stations, the teacher's role is to support the work in each station, observe the learning, and document observations.

Phase Two – Day Seven

Prepping for the day: Today the discovery learning will be focused on different bird feet and their specific uses. To plan for a successful day of learning, you'll want to gather close-up photographs of different bird feet, find an expert preschool/kids video on birds' feet, lay out a large sheet of white bulletin board paper with crayons, markers, colored pencils and any other art medium, and finally prewrite the project message.

Discovery Step #1: Invite students to the central meeting space and read the project message together. Pause and invite students to "share the pen" and add to the message with their drawings and letters. Share with students that they will be going outside for the last time today to observe birds and continue to record their observations.

Project Message Idea:
Nest builders,
Yesterday, you built a bird's nest.
What did you discover?
What's interesting about bird feet?

Discovery Step #2: Bring students outside with their field guides, binoculars, pencils, and clipboards for a final day of observing birds in their habitats. Once students have observed for a while, bring them back in to share new discoveries in the central meeting space.

Discovery Step #3: Lay out several photographs in the center of the meeting circle and invite students to notice and wonder as they look at the different pictures. Begin a class conversation about their observations.

Discovery Step #4: Read a book focusing on different birds' feet or watch an expert video about birds' feet. This knowledge will help students as they grow in their understanding of birds and what makes them special. Pose the question, "What is special about a bird's feet?" Have them turn their partner and share their thinking. Be sure to listen in on conversation and ask questions as they converse.

Discovery Step #5: Lay out the giant piece of bulletin board paper either on the floor or across a table. Invite students to consider all the different bird feet and their uses and draw them on the giant bird feet mural. Be sure to have the bird feet photographs on hand if students need to refer to a model for drawing. Also, as they draw the feet, question students on what the feet may be used for or important things that make them special. Record their responses on strips of paper and glue them near the feet drawn by the student. After the mural is complete, discuss the different feet, their features and uses with students. The mural should be hung in a central location in the classroom.

Inquiry Stations – Learners will move to their third round of stations. Groups should be rotating through a different inquiry station each day. Students should rotate with the same friends for the duration of the six days. You'll want to be sure to communicate each group's station for the day and where they'll rotate the next day. Students should be spending between 10 and 20 minutes in stations each day. Remember, during inquiry stations, the teacher's role is to support the work in each station, observe the learning and document observations.

Phase Two – Day Eight

Prepping for the day: Talking bird beaks and their uses is today's discovery focus. You'll want to be totally prepped for an incredible day of learning more about what makes a bird's beak special. In planning for learning, gather books about beaks, an expert video, or both. There is also a planned whole-class investigation where you'll test out the use of different bird beaks. You will need a few supplies for this investigation: an ice scoop, salad tongs, a bowl filled with cut brown yarn at the bottom, water mixed with coca power to mimic dirty pond water, goldfish, and rubber ducks. Be sure to create your project message before learning begins.

Discovery Step #1: Invite students to the central meeting space and read the project message together. Pause and invite students to "share the pen" and add to the message with their drawings and letters.

Project Message Idea:
Tweeting friends,
Why are birds' feet different?

Today we are investigating bird beaks. What do you think we'll find out?

Discovery Step #2: Lay out several photographs in the center of the meeting circle and invite students to notice and wonder as they look at the different pictures of bird beaks. Invite them to turn and talk with their partner about what they notice.

Discovery Step #3: In the central meeting space, read aloud book on bird beaks. Discuss with the students the different uses of bird beaks and their observations.

Discovery Step #4: On a table in the classroom, before students arrive, set up the bird beak class investigation. You'll want to have different pictures of beaks, along with a model of a pond and a grassy area, a large straining spoon to mimic a duck's beak, an ice scoop to mimic a pelican's beak, and fine motor tongs to mimic a crane's beak.

Pond Model Set-up: Take a container and lay pieces of yarn at the bottom to mimic worms, wrap green colored paper to mimic grass around the container, fill the container with a few goldfish crackers, then mix water and cocoa mix together to mimic muddy water, dump in muddy water in container over fish and yarn, then place rubber ducks on for the final pond model.

FIGURE 7.12 Discovery experiment set up to test out bird beaks.

Dirt and Grass Set Up: Take a second container and line the bottom with lots of cut brown yarn to mimic worms and possibly snakes, dump a bag of brown sugar over the top as dirt, then stick short pieces of green construction paper out of the sugar to act as blades of grass.

FIGURE 7.13 Discovery experiment set up to test out bird beaks.

Invite students to gather around the table for the investigation. Facilitate discussion on how they just read about the differences in bird beaks and their uses. Now, we're going to investigate to see exactly how they work. Visit each model and talk about the tool being used as the beak and how it's like a real bird's beak. Model how the duck's beak acts as a strainer straining out water and leaving in fish another bottom pond food. Invite different students to test out the duck's beak. Then move to the dirt and grass model and discuss with students the long shape of a crane's beak to dig its beak deep into the dirt and pull out worms, snakes, and other food. Let students test out different bird beaks and uncover their purpose and use.

FIGURE 7.14 Discovery experiment set up to test different types of bird beaks.

Stations – Learners will move to their fourth round of stations. Groups should be rotating through a different inquiry station each day. Students should be spending between 10 and 20 minutes in stations each day. Remember, during inquiry stations, the teacher's role is to support the work in each station, observe the learning and document observations.

Phase Two – Day Nine

Prepping for the day: Today we're talking bird sounds! Prior to the lesson, you'll want to gather a good bird sound video from the internet, images of bird movements, non-fiction bird books that either tell about the bird's sound or its movements.

Discovery Step #1: Invite students to the central meeting space and read the project message together. Pause and invite students to "share the pen" and add to the message with their drawings and letters.

> **Project Message Idea:**
> Bird Beaks of All Kinds,
> What did we discover about bird beaks?
> What do you know about the sounds birds make? Can you try to make one?

Discovery Step #2: Watch the selected expert video on bird sounds and movements. Talk with students about the differences in the sounds birds make.

Discovery Step #3: Practice the different bird sounds with learners. Cultivate a conversation around when birds use their calls and what they tell us.

Discovery Step #4: Read about four different birds and the specific movements they make. These excerpts can be found in various non-fiction bird books. Invite students to act out these bird movements. You might consider taking pictures of this in action for documentation and an addition to the focus wall.

Discovery Step #5: Make a chart with the students of the different bird movements and a drawn picture of the bird making that movement. Students can help with the drawings of these movements in action. Display this poster near the focus wall when complete.

Stations – Learners will move to their fifth round of stations. Groups should be rotating through a different inquiry station each day. Students should be spending between 10 and 20 minutes in stations each day. Remember, during inquiry stations, the teacher's role is to support the work in each station, observe the learning and document observations.

Phase Two – Day Ten

Prepping for the day: Today's learning will be centered around students working in groups to learn more about a specific type of bird. Each group of three or four students will work to research and display their knowledge of the bird on a fact poster. Groups will need pictures and books of specific bird types to support their research. (Group examples: hummingbirds, penguins, ducks, eagles, etc.) Groups will also need art supplies and a large sheet of paper for fact poster creation. The project message should be created before the learning begins.

Discovery Step #1: Invite students to the central meeting space and read the project message together. Pause and invite students to "share the pen" and add to the message with their drawings and letters.

> **Project Message Idea:**
> Bird Tweets of All Kinds,
> Why do birds have different calls?
> Are all birds the same?
> What is different about a hummingbird and an owl?

Discovery Step #2: Share an expert early childhood video on different types of birds. Engage in discussion about what makes birds different. Invite students to share ideas about different birds, where they've seen them, or what they discovered through the video.

Discovery Step #3: Place students in their groups around the classroom with sufficient room for working as a team. They should have all their materials (photography, books, art supplies, large sheet of paper, etc.) in their working location. Explain to students that they are going to research a specific type of bird, observe it through pictures, and create a fact poster about the bird to share with the rest of the class. As groups work together, walk around discussing information in the books with groups, asking important questions and supporting their thinking as they make meaning from the text and photographs.

FIGURE 7.15 Students investigating and displaying their knowledge on ducks through a drawing.

Discovery Step #4: Invite groups to share what they learned from their investigations and their fact posters. The posters can be hung around the room and photographed as documentation.

Stations – Learners will move to their sixth and final round of stations. Groups should be rotating to their last station today.

Phase Two – Day Eleven

Prepping for the day: Days eleven and twelve are the last two days of Phase Two. Across these two days, students will begin researching, completing their expert knowledge, and creating their final projects.

The Project: This culminating project has been designed to be a whole-class project, where each child individually contributes. We are building a bird museum! The museum will feature different types of birds created by the students. They will first select a favorite bird that have developed expert knowledge on, spend a day looking at pictures and reading more about the bird, then finishing with a constructed bird model. Each child will create one bird model over the next two days, and it will be placed in the class bird museum.

Discovery Step #1: Gather students into the central meeting space and talk about all the great learning they have done over the last two weeks. Then ask them to think about a bird that they've learned the most about and have lots of expert knowledge to share. Invite students to turn and talk to their neighbor about the bird they chose and expert knowledge about the bird.

Discovery Step #2: Explain to students that today begins the final project day where they will create a model of a bird to show their expert knowledge. Ask if anyone has ever been to a museum. Talk with them about museums. Share with learners that they will be working on a bird museum to share their knowledge with others.

Discovery Step #3: After each child has selected an expert bird, invite them to look through books and photographs to gain more expert knowledge on that specific bird. This should last for a while, as students dig through books and have conversations with each other. While they are finalizing their research, you'll want to question students on their bird of choice and their knowledge.

Discovery Step #4: Continue to explain that their museum display will have a drawing of their selected bird as well as a model they will create tomorrow with various art supplies. Pass out plan sheets of paper and invite students to paint, draw or color their bird of choice. Talk about including many of the details we've talked about over the last few days (birds' feather colors, type of beak, type of feet, body shape, use of feathers, habitat, etc.).

Phase Two – Day Twelve

Prepping for the day: This is the last day of Phase Two and an exciting one! Today students will use various art supplies and modeling clay to create their selected bird model for the bird museum. You'll want to consider the foundation (what they'll build their bird on) for their creation: brown craft box, paper plate, paper tray, etc.

Art Supplies to Support Culminating Project:

- ◆ Modeling dough
- ◆ Assortment of colored feathers
- ◆ Wiggle eyes
- ◆ Paper shapes
- ◆ Popsicle sticks
- ◆ Yarn
- ◆ Buttons
- ◆ Pom pom balls
- ◆ Paper straws
- ◆ Foundation for bird: plate, tray, box, etc.

Discovery Step #1: Have the table/working space set up for bird creating. You may consider having all the supplies set out in the center of the table with the base ready at each spot.

FIGURE 7.16 The table is prepped for culminating projects to show expert knowledge.

Discovery Step #2: Invite experts to find a spot around the bird exhibit creation table to begin bringing their birds to life. Students will use a variety of materials to create their bird. Encourage their creations with questions about their bird and observations about the details they include.

FIGURE 7.17 Students are displaying expert knowledge of birds for their culminating bird museum project.

FIGURE 7.18 A student used expert knowledge to create a bird for the final project.

FIGURE 7.19 A model of a parrot created for final bird museum project. Student has used expert knowledge to create model for presentation day.

> **Discovery Step #3:** After bird experts have finalized their bird creations, students will label their bird and place it in the class bird museum. After all birds have been finished, the students love going up to view the models and share ideas with each other.

A View of the Final Bird Museum Culminating Project

FIGURE 7.20 The culminating project display – A bird museum.

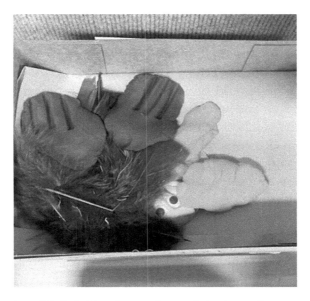

FIGURE 7.21 A model of a bald eagle created as a culminating project.

Phase Three – Celebrate and Share

The planned duration for Phase Three (the celebration phase) is two days. During these two days, students will plan their project celebration, before presenting their expert knowledge on the final day.

TABLE 7.3
Layout planning for phase three of bird unit

Phase Three	Day 13	2 Discovery Steps
	Day 14	1 Discovery Step

Phase Three Suggested Materials:

♦ Art supplies – crayons, markers, colored pencils, paint, etc.
♦ Paper for invitation creation
♦ Backdrop creation supplies – bulletin board paper, paint, etc.

Phase Three – Day Thirteen

Prepping for the day: Today is all about letting the students planning and creativity shine! As a class, they will determine who should be invited, where the presentations will take place and what expert knowledge they plan on sharing. The teachers' work will consist of gathering samples of student documentation (photographs of students at work, work samples, etc.) to put on display.

Discovery Step #1: Gather students together to collaborate on a few ideas:

1. Who should be invited to the presentation day tomorrow?
2. Who will make the invitations?
3. What important information should be placed on the invitation?
4. Where will the presentations take place?
5. Will there be a stage or a backdrop?
6. What order will bird experts present?

Once these questions have been decided upon, students will break into groups to get busy working on the invitations, stage set up, display areas and the backdrop.

Discovery Step #2: Send groups of students to deliver the invitations to the invited guests. If by chance the guests are not part of the school faculty, you can snap a quick picture of the invitation and email it.

Phase Three – Day Fourteen

Prepping for the day: Today is a celebration of all the wonderful learning that has taken place over the last two weeks in the PBL unit on birds! Students will take turns presenting their bird models and sharing their expert knowledge with classmates and invited guests. Refer back to the end of chapter four for a more detailed view of the celebration day.

Discovery Step #1: As invited guests arrive and students take their places in the audience, the presentations will begin.

Each speaker will have the opportunity to share their expert knowledge, answer questions from the audience and share their bird model.

Once all students have presented their bird models and expert knowledge, invite students to share their learning around the room with the invited guests.

After the project has concluded, consider displaying the learning somewhere in your hallway, front office or another school location to share the newly learned knowledge with others. Students from around the school will now have the opportunity to grow their knowledge of birds through the class display.

Unit Two: Neighborhoods
Project Based Learning Unit Sampler 2
Project Topic – Neighborhoods
Timeline: 18 days

Overview: In the project-based unit on neighborhoods, students will explore the different facets of a neighborhood by discovering more about the unique people, places and things found within each neighborhood.

Driving Question: What is a neighborhood?

Picture books to support all three phases throughout unit:

- *People in My Neighborhood* by Shelly Lyons (2013)
- *Signs in My Neighborhood* by Shelly Lyons (2013)
- *City Signs* by Zoran Milich (2005)
- *We Love Reading Street Signs* by Dustin Lee Carlton (2017)
- *On My Block* by Zeta Elliott (2020)
- *Helpers in Your Neighborhood* by Shira Evans (2018)
- *Good Morning, Neighbor* by Davide Cali (2018)
- *Places in My Neighborhood* by Shelly Lyons (2013)
- *In Lucia's Neighborhood* by Pat Shewchuk (2013)
- *Who's Hat is This?* by Sharon Cooper (2006)
- *Meet a Mail Carrier!* by Becky Herrick (2021)
- *Last Stop on Market Street* by Matt de la Pena (2015)

◆ *In Every House on Every Street* by Jess Hitchman (2019)
◆ *Map My Neighborhood* by Jennifer Boothroyd (2013)
◆ *Homes for Everyone* by Jennifer Gillis (2006)

Phase One – An Immersion into Learning More about Neighborhoods

The planned duration for Phase One (the immersion phase) is three days. During these three days of immersion, students will be introduced to the places and parts of a neighborhood, discover neighborhood maps, and display their prior knowledge about a neighborhood. During Phase One, the teacher will begin observing and documenting the learning of each child as they progress through the unit. The documentation log from Chapter 6 is

TABLE 7.4
Three-day plan for Phase One in PBL unit on neighborhoods

Phase One	Day 1	4 Discovery Steps
	Day 2	3 Discovery Steps
	Day 3	4 Discovery Steps

a great place to begin.
Phase One Materials:

◆ Collection of picture books on neighborhoods, community helpers, places in a neighborhood, neighborhood signs
◆ Real photographs of a variety of neighborhood pictures (places, signs, streets, people)
◆ Chart paper
◆ Selected spot for focus wall
◆ Topic (Neighborhoods) labeled at the top of focus wall
◆ Magnifying glasses
◆ Simple neighborhood maps for viewing
◆ Neighborhood play items – train set, playhouses, play people, small cars, street signs, anything you have on hand

Phase One – Day One

Prepping for the day: Before students enter the room on day one, you'll want to have the beginnings of your focus wall set up and in place. This includes a title-Neighborhoods, photographs hanging around the wall, and a neighborhoods can/have/are chart.

Discovery Step #1: The PBL unit on neighborhoods will begin with a focused book reading. Gather students together and read aloud a book on neighborhoods. Stop throughout the reading and model thinking out loud about things you notice in the book.

Sample Think-Aloud – "Wow! I see that there are a lot of different places and people in a neighborhood. This page shows a restaurant where people eat and there is a restaurant in my neighborhood too."

Discovery Step #2: A gallery walk of neighborhood pictures – Hang up various neighborhood photographs around the room and invite students to walk with their partner around the room visiting each photograph and stopping to chat about what they notice. You might consider playing classical or low music as they walk and share. While students are conversing during the gallery walk, you can listen in on conversations and begin documenting their ideas and wonders.

Discovery Step #3: Invite students back to the central meeting area to share ideas about what they noticed in the gallery walk. Direct their attention to the Neighborhoods Can/Have/Are chart and ask them to begin sharing what neighborhoods can, have, and are. Write their ideas on the chart and consider inviting a few friends to come up and draw or write their ideas about what neighborhoods can give or provide. Continue to document their ideas on the chart, as well as invite them to come up and add their own ideas to the chart.

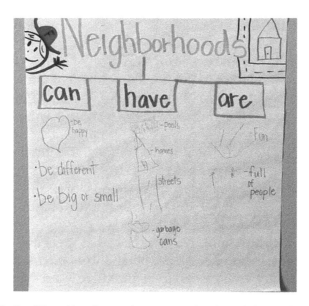

FIGURE 7.22 Can/Have/Are chart to document student knowledge in phase one.

Discovery Step #4: Bringing day one to a close – Invite students to draw a picture of a neighborhood on plain paper. As you pass out the paper, remind them to fill up the entire page with ideas. This will give you a glimpse into their understanding of a neighborhood and their misconceptions.

Phase One – Day Two

Prepping for the day: Today, we'll focus on writing down our wonders about neighborhoods and discover more about neighborhoods through play. Before today's learning begins, you'll want to have the chart hanging with the title – "What do you wonder about neighborhoods?"

Discovery Step #1: Today's neighborhood learning will begin by gathering students to the central meeting space to chat about and document wonders about neighborhoods on the wonder chart. Ask students to turn to their buddy and share their what they may wonder about neighborhoods. As students share their wonders, document thinking, and conversations on the class wonder chart. This chart will hang on the focus wall for the duration of the unit. As the unit progresses, students will discover answers to the questions and answer them.

Discovery Step #2: Select a book from the book display on neighborhoods and read aloud to students. As you read, stop and notice things that are included in a neighborhood.

Discovery Step #3: Discovery through play – It's time to observe our students through play to see what information they are connecting when thinking about a neighborhood. Place several building opportunities for students and invite them to build a neighborhood and play.

Possible Neighborhood Discovery Play Ideas:

♦ Blocks
♦ Train sets with train tracks
♦ Small houses
♦ Buildings
♦ Connecting blocks
♦ People figurines
♦ Animals
♦ Toy trees
♦ Play street signs
♦ Anything that might contribute to neighborhood play

Phase One – Day Three

Prepping for the day: In today's learning, students will gain a better understanding of a neighborhood map. After viewing and discussing different maps, the entire class will create a large map on bulletin board paper. The map will feature streets and bridges and each day for the rest of the unit, a new idea will be added to the class neighborhood map.

Suggested Book: *Map My Neighborhood* by Jennifer Boothroyd (2013)

Discovery Step #1: Read aloud of a book on neighborhood maps (see book suggestion above). As you read, pause and point out different things in the book. Chat about what maps do and how they help us.

Discovery Step #2: After the book discussion has come to a close, place simple map pictures in the center of the meeting circle or scattered on tables around the room. Invite students to notice and wonder as they observe the simple maps.

Discovery Step #3: Place a large sheet of bulletin board paper on the floor or across a few tables in the classroom. Explain to students that they are going to create a giant map of a neighborhood and add a few things to it each day as they learn more about neighborhoods. Today, they will begin by designing the streets and bridges in the neighborhood. Invite students to plan, draw, and color or paint the streets and bridges of the classroom neighborhood map. Remember, it's important to let them take the lead in designing this map.

FIGURE 7.23 A neighborhood map created by early childhood students.

Discovery Step #4: After the streets on the neighborhood map have been completed, invite students back to the central meeting space to begin the ABC neighborhood chart. The chart should be premade with 26 boxes. Ask the students to come up and fill in the alphabet with one letter going in each box. Then, invite students to begin brainstorming a list of things that relate to neighborhoods and place them under the correct letter. This is a great way to organize information. This chart will be revisited each day throughout the remainder of the unit as new words and ideas come up.

FIGURE 7.24 ABC chart to organize information throughout the three phases of the PBL unit on neighborhoods.

Phase Two – Discovery, Inquiry and Innovation

The planned duration for Phase Two (the inquiry phase) is seven days, beginning with day 4 of the unit and lasting until day 10. The next seven days will be packed with inquiry, discovery, investigations, stations, and project creations. Students will discover more about a neighborhood through field site visits, virtual field trips, class investigations, inquiry station visits, and finish with project creations. During Phase Two, the teacher will provide discovery opportunities, observe learners, and document the learning and support learners in creating a model to share their expert knowledge of things in a neighborhood.

TABLE 7.5

Table displays the planning and discovery phases in
Phase Two of the PBL unit on neighborhoods

Phase Two	Day 4	5 Discovery Steps
	Day 5	4 Discovery Steps
	Day 6	5 Discovery Steps
	Day 7	4 Discovery Steps
	Day 8	5 Discovery Steps
	Day 9	3 Discovery Steps
	Day 10	5 Discovery Steps
	Day 11	2 Inquiry Station Visits
	Day 12	2 Inquiry Station Visits
	Day 13	2 Inquiry Station Visits
	Day 14	4 Discovery Steps
	Day 15	2 Discovery Steps
	Day 16	2 Discovery Steps

Phase Two Suggested Materials:

◆ Collection of picture books on neighborhoods on display
  in the room
◆ Real photographs of neighborhoods, community helpers,
  places in a neighborhood, street signs
◆ Chart paper
◆ Items and playthings for setting up a restaurant (fake
  food, plates, etc.)
◆ Community helper hats and dress up items
◆ White bulletin board paper
◆ Paint/paintbrushes
◆ Chart paper
◆ Loose parts (Daly et al., 2014)
◆ Large, printed neighborhood signs

Note – additional materials are needed for inquiry stations and
the culminating project. Materials are listed in the correlating
pages following.

Phase Two – Day Four

Prepping for the day: The first day of Phase Two opens with a project message for students to help construct using their prior knowledge. Students will also discover further about families that live in a neighborhood. The first piece to the neighborhood map will be constructed today as each student adds a drawing of their family's home.

Discovery Step #1: Today, students will begin the second phase with a project message. Gather students to the central meeting space to read and construct parts of the message together.

> **Project Message Idea:**
> Hi Neighbors,
> Yesterday we created a giant map of neighborhood streets, grass and bridges.
> What else should we add to our neighborhood map?
> What do you find in a neighborhood?

Discovery Step #2: Invite students to turn and talk about things they do with their families in their neighborhood. You may consider modeling this conversation to help students form thoughts and ideas.

Sample Think-Aloud: In my neighborhood we have a park and a community pool. On Saturday afternoons, our family walks to the park and we slide down the slide together. I see many friends at the neighborhood park, and we talk and play. After we play for a while, we take a swim in the neighborhood pool.

Discovery Step #3: After thinking and talking more about neighborhoods, read a story about different homes in neighborhoods. Open the discussion by inviting students to share more about the home they live in.

Read-Aloud Suggestion: *Homes for Everyone* by Jennifer Gillis (2006)

Discovery Step #4: Pass out plain sheets of paper and tell students to spend time thinking about their own home and family. Ask them to use all the space on the paper to draw their house and their family. Encourage them to include as many details as possible in their drawing.

Discovery Step #5: After all drawings are complete, bring students over to the community map painting. Begin discussion about what would happen if all their pictures were added to the map. We want them to begin seeing that many homes begin making a neighborhood. Invite students to use tape and other supplies to add their picture to the map.

FIGURE 7.25 A student-created home and family for the class neighborhood map.

Phase Two – Day Five

Prepping for the day: Today the learning will be centered on places we find in a neighborhood. Students will brainstorm different places found in a neighborhood and why each place is an important addition to a neighborhood.

An important place in a neighborhood will be brought to life through dramatic play.

Discovery Step #1: In today's learning, students will gain a deeper understanding of the important places that are found in a neighborhood. Begin by gathering students to the central meeting space for a read aloud on neighborhood places. You'll want to select a book that highlights the different places found in a neighborhood (restaurants, schools, grocery stores, an ice cream shop, post office, etc.). As you read, stop and discuss the different places in the book.

Discovery Step #2: In order for students to have a first-hand look at places in a neighborhood, consider taking them on a walk around the outside of the school building as a field study. Are there any places near your school that are visible from the building? If not, a virtual field trip around a neighborhood is a great alternative option. Also, consider asking parents to take their child on a scavenger hunt after school. Extend the idea that, as a family, they can ride around the neighborhood and notice places as they ride. This is a great way to involve parents in the learning too!

Discovery Step #3: Invite students to think about important places in the neighborhood and begin drafting a list to hang on the concept wall. Ask students to pick one important neighborhood place to bring to life in the classroom. Explain that, as a class, students will design a space in the room to look like an actual place in a neighborhood. The dramatic set up and play experience will be a whole-class learning opportunity. Once the students have selected an important neighborhood place, they'll begin designing the area to bring it to life with props and furniture movement. We want their creativity to soar in this play experience! For example, if the selected place were a restaurant, students would use various items in the room to set up the restaurant dramatic play space. Then allow them time to play and try on different roles in the restaurant.

Discovery Step #4: After students have created the dramatic play area and played in various roles there, bring them back to the central meeting space for conversation. Invite students to share more about their experience in bringing a place in a neighborhood to life in the classroom. Use this as an opportunity to document their thoughts and ideas.

Phase Two – Day Six

Prepping for the day: The learning about places found in a neighborhood will continue today with new opportunities for learning. The day will begin with a project message and move into extended opportunities for discovery. Students will track their knowledge on a bubble map, then work in a group to create a model of a neighborhood place to add to the class neighborhood map.

Discovery Step #1: Gather students to the central meeting space and read the project message aloud. Invite students to share ideas and help create ideas to add to the project message.

Project Message Idea:
Hello Neighbor,
Yesterday we discovered more about places we find in a neighborhood.
What did we create yesterday? Why is this place important?

Discovery Step #2: If it's not possible to visit a place in the neighborhood surrounding the school, offer a virtual field study to the class. There are a variety of online videos for early childhood students that take them on a tour of different places in a neighborhood.

Discovery Step #3: Create a bubble map with the title – "Places in our Neighborhood." Invite students to draw and add to the bubble map the different places in neighborhoods along with the service they provide to the neighborhood. Example: Fire station – Firetrucks, firefighters, and safety.

Discovery Step #4: Explain to students that they are going to work in either groups of two or three to use loose parts (Daly et al., 2014) to create a place in a neighborhood.

After the creations are finished, each group will add their place to the neighborhood map. Groups should also label their place on the map with a handwritten sign. For the discovery creation, you may consider having photographs of neighborhood places printed for reference, books pulled, and other inquiry materials on hand. Once groups have been established, students will begin by researching their neighborhood place through reading and observing photographs. Following the research, students will create a plan, gather loose part materials, and begin building.

Discovery Step #5: Once groups have finished their loose parts creation of a place found in a community, allow opportunities for groups to share as they secure it to the neighborhood map.

Phase Two – Day Seven

Prepping for the day: Today's learning will allow for discovery on different helpers found in neighborhoods (firefighters, teachers, garbage collectors, mail carriers, vets, etc.). The learning will begin with a thoughtful project message and lead into discovery opportunities for students to learn more about the helpers in a neighborhood.

Discovery Step #1: Invite students to gather into the central meeting space to collaborate on the project message.

> **Project Message Idea:**
> Dear Neighborhood Helper,
> How do you help others?
> Who are people in your neighborhood that help others?

Discovery Step #2: Read a story aloud to students about neighborhood helpers or provide a virtual learning opportunity which introduces helpers in a neighborhood. Begin conversing with students about helpers and the tools they use to do their job.

Discovery Step #3: Dramatic play opportunity – Gather any kind of community helper costumes, artifacts, etc. and place them in center circle or around the room. Invite students to try on their uniforms and pretend to be a helper in the neighborhood. Provide opportunities for them to use the helper tools and uncover what they are used for in various jobs. Snap pictures of students as they act out various helper roles. These photographs will serve as great documentation. Hang them on the focus wall with a caption describing the activity and learning.

Discovery Step #4: Place community helper books around the classroom. Students will visit different areas of the room and discover more about different helpers, as they chat with each other about the information they are reading. Are they uncovering any answers from the wonder chart? These findings should be discussed and documented on the focus wall. This is also a perfect time to document their learning and conversations in your documentation binder.

Phase Two – Day Eight

Prepping for the day: Discovering more about helpers around neighborhoods will continue today. A project message will begin the learning, followed by a mural of neighborhood helpers and their special tools to demonstrate students' knowledge.

Discovery Step #1: Gather students to the central meeting space in the classroom and begin reading and composing the project message together.

> **Project Message Idea:**
> Greetings Neighbor,
> Yesterday we met and talked about helpers in our neighborhood.
> How do mail carriers help in the neighborhood?

Discovery Step #2: Share a virtual field trip video, plan a Zoom meeting, or invite a neighborhood helper to visit and share more about their job. This will help students as they gain real-life perspectives of the jobs helpers have around the neighborhood.

Discovery Step #3: Create the opportunity for students to discover many neighborhood helpers by playing the neighborhood helpers guessing game.

How to play:

1. Print neighborhood helper pictures on small cards
2. Call one student up to the center of the circle and have him/her place a neighborhood helper card from the pile on their forehead
3. Invite the rest of the students to give clues about the neighborhood helper for the guessing student to guess which helper is on their card
4. Allow students to take turns being the guesser

Discovery Step #4: Lay out a large sheet of white bulletin board paper across a table or on the floor of the classroom. Share with students that they are going to create a neighborhood helper mural. Each student will choose one neighborhood helper to paint on the mural. Students will be working from different locations on the mural; have enough supplies ready for their work. Consider encouraging them to paint the tools that their helper uses in their job on the mural too.

Discovery Step #5: Give students the opportunity to share more about the neighborhood helper they chose to create on the mural.

Phase Two – Day Nine

Prepping for the day: Today students will display their knowledge of neighborhood helpers by once again using loose parts to create a neighborhood helper for the classroom neighborhood map.

Discovery Step #1: Invite students to the central meeting space to create a song about one neighborhood helper through a project message.

> **Project Message Idea:**
> Hi Helper,
> We've talked about many different helpers that work in our neighborhoods.
> Create a song about a neighborhood helper that tells about their job and the tools they use.

Discovery Step #2: Share another virtual field trip about a neighborhood helper or invite a neighborhood helper to come and share more about their job. Give opportunities for students to ask questions to the invited neighborhood helper.

Discovery Step #3: Place an abundance of loose parts (Daly et al., 2014) on tables around the room and invite students to use their knowledge of a neighborhood helper to create one helper. You might also consider having photographs of neighborhood helpers and books readily available for research during the creation.

Ideas for loose parts to create community workers:

Popsicle sticks, pom pom balls, wiggly eyes, felt squares of different colors, yarn, odds and ends from around the room, etc.

Phase Two – Day Ten

Prepping for the day: Today students will discover more about important signs around neighborhoods and their messages. Students will notice the shapes of different signs and create them with various materials.

Discovery Step #1: Begin with the shared project message experience in the central meeting location in the classroom.

> **Project Message Idea:**
> What is red with four giant letters that say "S..T..O..P"?
> What signs do you see around your neighborhood?

Discovery Step #2: Place photographs of various neighborhood signs on the floor in the center of the central meeting space circle. Invite students to notice things about the various sign photographs. Listen in on their discussions with each other as they notice and wonder.

Support students in discussing:

The shape of each sign

The color of each sign

The information each sign displays

Discovery Step #3: Using various materials, give students the opportunity to create different sign shapes. This provides students with the opportunity to develop an understanding of shapes and their attributes.

Material Ideas: Popsicle sticks, yarn, straws, etc.

Discovery Step #4: Bring students to the class neighborhood map. Pair them with a buddy and ask them to look carefully at the map and consider where a sign may be needed. Provide materials for students to work with a buddy to create one sign to add to the community map. Materials that may be considered: molding clay, paper, crayons, paint, cardboard, etc.

Discovery Step #5: After all sign projects have been completed, students will secure their sign on the neighborhoods map. As they place it on the map, ask them to share more about their plan for creation.

Inquiry Stations

Continuing on in days 11–13, students begin rotating through the six stations. Students should be placed in inquiry station rotation groups and each group will visit two stations over the course of three days. They will visit all six stations in the three-day time frame. During the three inquiry station days, students will only visit stations; there will be no formal whole-group learning on these days. In order to prepare and prep the inquiry stations, you'll need to gather materials for each station, set them up in various locations around the room, and leave them up for the duration of the three days. Each station will contain its own materials, and a station guide, including a driving question and activity. Consider looking at your class list and making a rotation schedule with groups of four or five students. You'll want to keep track of who visited each station throughout the three days, so rotations maintain a smooth flow.

Station One: Neighborhood Storytelling
Storytelling Station Materials:

- ◆ People figurines
- ◆ Neighborhood building pieces (train tracks, buildings, blocks)
- ◆ Photographs of neighborhood maps, neighborhood helpers and buildings
- ◆ Picture books to support neighborhood helpers

Inquiry Station Set Up: Choose a location in the classroom to set up this station. Set out building materials, figurines, photographs, etc. Create a station guide which includes a wonder question and explains to students the possibilities for discovery.
Suggestions for Station Guide:

1. How do people work together in a neighborhood?
2. Make up a neighborhood story using the people and building materials.

Inquiry Station Experience: The neighborhood storytelling station is all about bringing neighbors together through storytelling. Students will create a story in a neighborhood setting using building blocks and figurines. This provides them with the opportunity to see how all the pieces and parts of a neighborhood work together.

Station Two: Dramatic Play – A Post Office
Post Office Station Materials:

- ◆ Photographs of a post office
- ◆ Virtual field trip video on iPad on postal office workers
- ◆ Picture books about postal workers
- ◆ Materials for setting up a post office

Cardboard boxes
Markers/paint
Paper
Envelopes
Anything that would add to the play experience

Inquiry Station Set Up: Choose a location in the classroom to set up this station. Set out photographs of a post office, books, and building materials, along with a station guide. Suggestions for Station Guide:

1. What does a post office look like?
2. Who works in a post office?
3. Work with your group to create and play in a post office.

Inquiry Station Experience: Students will bring a post office to life through planning, setting up, and dramatic play. They will use their knowledge of a post office and its workers to create their own working post office in the classroom. Since this station will be visited by six rotation groups, each group will have the opportunity to add to prior set up and play from the previous groups.

Station Three: Neighborhood Helper Books
Book Writing Station Materials:

- ◆ Picture books on helpers in the neighborhood
- ◆ Paper
- ◆ Stapler
- ◆ Markers, colored pencils, pencils, etc.
- ◆ Station guide

Inquiry Station Set Up: Choose a location in the classroom with a table to support book illustrating and writing. Set out a variety of illustration materials, papers and the station guide.
Suggestions for Station Guide:
1. What story can you tell about a neighborhood?
2. Use the materials to write and illustrate a book.

Inquiry Station Experience: The book-making station is all about learning to tell a story or write an informational text which involves a neighborhood. In this station, students will demonstrate their knowledge through authoring a book. Various papers and supplies will allow them to freely plan and create their own stories.

Station Four: Dramatic Play – A Bakery

FIGURE 7.26 A student plays at the bakery dramatic play inquiry station.

Bakery Station Materials:

- ◆ Photographs of a bakery
- ◆ Video on iPad for early childhood on a bakery or a baker
- ◆ Picture books about bakeries
- ◆ Materials for setting up a bakery
    Cardboard boxes
    Play food, plates, etc.
    Paper, markers, colored pencils
    Cash register, play money
    Anything that would add to the play experience

Inquiry Station Set Up: Choose a location in the classroom to set up this station. Set out photographs of different bakeries, books, and creation materials. Also create a station guide that explains to students what they will be discovering in that station.

Suggestions for Station Guide:

1. Why do neighborhoods have bakeries?
2. Who works in a bakery?
3. What is sold in a bakery?
4. Work with your group to create a bakery and play.

Inquiry Station Experience: This station is about learning through play! Students have an up-close experience in setting up and carrying out different roles in a bakery. Each group has the opportunity to add to the bakery set up and pretend to work and shop in the bakery. Be as creative as you can with suppling enough materials for students to use their imaginations and knowledge to bring a real neighborhood bakery to life in the classroom.

FIGURE 7.27 This child is learning through play in the dramatic play inquiry station.

Station Five: Drawing Neighborhood Maps

Map-Making Station Materials:

- ◆ Photographs of simple neighborhood maps
- ◆ Large sheets of paper
- ◆ Materials for drawing and creating maps
  Crayons
  Markers
  Paint
  Paintbrushes

Inquiry Station Set Up: The best location for this station is a table. Display pictures of simple maps, along with the station guide and materials for drawing. Since students have been working on a whole-class neighborhood map, this offers a great opportunity to assess learning.
Suggestions for Station Guide:

1. What have you discovered about neighborhood maps?
2. Create your own neighborhood map.
3. What people, places, and signs will you draw?

Inquiry Station Experience: Calling all creators! This is the time for our little neighborhood map makers to use their imagination and knowledge from this PBL unit to bring their very own neighborhood map to life. Teacher questions should support them in considering:

1. What will the roads look like?
2. What important people and places will be found in the town?
3. What is the town's name?
4. How will people in the town work together?

Station Six: Telling a Helping Hands Story with Stop Motion Video

Station Materials:

- ◆ iPad with stop motion video application loaded
- ◆ People figurines

- ◆ Building blocks
- ◆ Paper
- ◆ Markers/colored pencils

Inquiry Station Set Up: The best location for this station is a table for background creation and stop motion video production.
Suggestions for Station Guide:

1. How do neighbors help each other?
2. Why is it important to show kindness to others?
3. Work with your team to create a movie about neighbors helping each other.

Inquiry Station Experience: Stop motion videos are a fantastic way for even our smallest learners to discover how small parts work together to make a whole story. In their movie-making role, students will design a movie set, discuss a small script, choose characters, and put it all together with the stop motion video creation.

If you are uncomfortable with the stop motion video creation station, an alternative option is another dramatic play experience.
Alternative Dramatic Play Ideas:

- ◆ Grocery Store
- ◆ Restaurant
- ◆ Fire Station

Phase Two – Day Fourteen

Prepping for the day: Today is all about project research and design. Students will choose how they plan to display their expert knowledge with the culminating project. Students can choose to work in groups, pairs, or individually to create and display their expert knowledge on neighborhoods. Students will research in books, investigate expert photos, and watch expert videos on select topics.

The Project: The culminating project is designed for students to work in pairs, groups, or individually. The goal in this project is to bring an aspect of the neighborhood to life.

Project Examples:

- ♦ A skit of firefighters helping a neighbor
- ♦ A model of a neighborhood map, including all the people and places
- ♦ A book about a veterinarian helping animals in the neighborhood

Refer to back to the end of Chapter 4 for additional ideas to support student projects. Looking back over documentation notes is another way to support students as they consider how they will display their expert knowledge.

Discovery Step #1: Gather students into the central meeting space and talk about all the great learning they have done in learning more about neighborhoods. Then ask them to think about a part of a neighborhood that they've learned the most about and have lots of expert knowledge to share. Invite students to turn and talk to their neighbor about areas of expertise.

Discovery Step #2: Explain to students that today is the final project day, where they will display their expert knowledge. Support students in considering how they would like to demonstrate their expert knowledge. Allow time to finalize research and design expert knowledge creation.

Discovery Step #3: After each child selects how they will display their expert knowledge, invite students to look through books and photographs to gain even more expert knowledge. While they are finalizing their research, support student thinking by questioning them about their neighborhood expert knowledge project plan.

Discovery Step #4: Pass out paper for students to brainstorm ideas and consider needed supplies for the next day's build.

Phase Two – Days Fifteen and Sixteen

Prepping for the day: These are the last two days of Phase Two. Today students will use various art supplies, technology, paper, or decided materials to bring their project plan and expert knowledge to life. Supplies should be easily accessible for students to gather as they begin the creation process.

Discovery Step #1: Have working spaces ready for students to begin assembling their expert knowledge creations. Depending on the type of creation they are building will depend on the amount of workspace needed.

Discovery Step #2: Invite students to gather their materials at the materials table and use their plan from yesterday to begin their expert knowledge project build. Creation time allows for strong documentation, as well an opportunity for teacher questioning. Students will have two full days to build their project creation; this includes assembling, writing, painting, etc. At the end of day two, all projects should be ready for presentations.

Phase Three – Celebrate and Share

The planned duration for Phase Three (the celebration phase) is two days. During these two days, students will plan their project celebration and present their expert knowledge.

TABLE 7.6

Table displays the planning and discovery phases in Phase Three of the PBL unit on neighborhoods

Phase Three	Day 17	3 Discovery Steps
	Day 18	1 Discovery Step

Phase Three Suggested Materials:

◆ Art supplies – crayons, markers, colored pencils, paint, etc.
◆ Paper for invitation creation
◆ Backdrop creation supplies – bulletin board paper, paint, etc.

Phase Three – Day Seventeen

Prepping for the day: Today is all about letting the students planning and creativity shine! As a class, they will determine who should be invited, where the presentations will take place, and what expert knowledge they plan on sharing. The teachers work will consist of gathering samples of student documentation (photographs of students at work, work samples, etc.) to put on display.

Discovery Step #1: Gather students together to collaborate on a few ideas:

1. Who should be invited to the presentation day tomorrow?
2. Who will make the invitations?
3. What important information should be placed on the invitation?
4. Where will the presentations take place?
5. Will there be a stage or a backdrop?
6. What order will bird experts present?

Once these questions have been decided upon, students will break into groups to get busy working on the invitations, stage set up, display areas, and the backdrop.

Discovery Step #2: Send groups of students to deliver the invitations to the invited guests. If, by chance, the guests are not part of the school faculty, you can snap a quick picture of the invitation and email it.

Phase Three – Day Eighteen

Prepping for the day: Today is a celebration of all the wonderful learning that has taken place over the last few weeks in the PBL unit on neighborhoods! Students take turns presenting their displays of expert knowledge with classmates and invited guests. Refer back to the end of Chapter 4 for a more detailed view of the celebration day.

Discovery Step #1: As invited guests arrive and students take their places in the audience, the presentations should begin. Each speaker will have the opportunity to share their expert knowledge, answer questions from the audience, and share their neighborhood creation.

After project presentations are finished, consider displaying the learning somewhere in your hallway, front office, or another school location to share the newly learned knowledge with others. Students from around the school will now have the opportunity to grow their knowledge of neighborhoods through the class display.

Further Reading

Daly, L., Beloglovsky, M., & Daly, J. (2014). *Loose Parts: Inspiring Play in Young Children (Loose Parts Series)* (Illustrated ed.). Redleaf Press.

Chapter 7 Picture Book Reference List

Boring, M., & Garrow, L. (1998). *Birds, Nests, and Eggs (Turtleback Binding Edition)* (Turtleback Binding ed.). Turtleback.

Cali, D., & Dek, M. (2018). *Good Morning Neighbor: (Picture Book on Sharing, Kindness, and Working as a Team, Ages 4–8)* (Illustrated ed.). Princeton Architectural Press.

Collard, S. B., III, & Brickman, R. (2002). *Beaks!* (Illustrated ed.). Charlesbridge.

Cole, H. (2021). *Nesting*. Katherine Tegen Books.

Cooper, K. S., & Muehlenhardt, A. B. (2006). *Whose Hat Is This?: A Look at Hats Workers Wear– Hard, Tall, and Shiny (Whose Is It?: Community Workers)* (Illustrated ed.) Picture Window Books.

Cousins, L. (2018). *Hooray for Birds!* (Illustrated ed.). Candlewick.

Donovan, L., & Paras, D. (2021). *Birds in My Backyard*. Independently Published.

Elliott, Z., & Wong, P. (2020). *On My Block*. Independently Published.

Evans, S. (2018). *National Geographic Readers: Helpers in Your Neighborhood (Pre-reader)* (Illustrated ed.). National Geographic Kids.

Garland, M. (2019). *Birds Make Nests* (Illustrated ed.). Holiday House.

Henkes, K., & Dronzek, L. (2017). *Birds Board Book* (Illustrated ed.). Greenwillow Books.

Hitchman, J., & Baleine, L. L. (2019). *In Every House on Every Street* (Illustrated ed.). Tiger Tales.

Hughes, C. (2016). *National Geographic Little Kids First Big Book of Birds (National Geographic Little Kids First Big Books)* (Illustrated ed.). National Geographic Kids.

Jenkins, P. B., & Rockwell, L. (2015). *A Nest Full of Eggs (Let's-Read-and-Find-Out Science 1)* (Illustrated ed.). HarperCollins.

De la Peña, M. (2016). *Last Stop On Market Street*. Penguin.

Lyons, S., & Saunders-Smith, G. (2013). *People in My Neighborhood*. Capstone Press.

Stewart, M. (2022). *Feathers: Not Just for Flying*. Charlesbridge.

Milton Keynes UK
Ingram Content Group UK Ltd.
UKHW021907310823
427871UK00024B/285